The Master Managers Handbook

Keys to Life
From the Garden

by

Patrick Barber Sr.
AUTHOR and PUBLISHER

STANLEY NC 28164

WEBSITE
www.one24now.com

PHONE
877-938-8853

EMAIL
mastermanagershandbook@gmail.com

AUTHORS EMAIL
pbarber1014@gmail.com

ISBN# 978-0-578-99624-0 eBook
ISBN# 978-0-578-99623-3 Paperback
ISBN# 978-0-578-33566-7 Hardcover

From the garden,

I attribute this book to My parents, Parks Sr., Hattie Barber, my oldest Brother Parks Jr, and my other Brother Elvis; all have journeyed home to be with our Lord and Savior. My (Wife) Tonya, (Daughter) Kennedy, (Sons) Patrick ll (Lanisha), Hamilton (Shanaya), Matthew (Khrystal), Kingsley, and my nephew, who we raised as ours, Jory Johnson. My Grandchildren, Samara, Ryann, Matthew ll, Marie, Khrystian, Glendia, Patrick J, and Harrison. My Sister Linda (John) Dawkins, William (Doris), Findley, and Perry. Haywood and Diane Phifer, Kisha and Will Phifer, Deyvonne Cunningham, Mazhin Q. Bego and Kendrix J. Penn.

My friends for life, Pastor Benjamin Murdock, James Harris-Mt Pleasant Baptist CH. Calvin Miller is known as Kool-Aid, JD and Joan Heath (NC), Dr. Eugene Gay, Richard and Claudia Howard (NC), Bruce Scoggins, and his wonderful Wife (NC). Alvin Bush and Karen (ATL), Willie, Rose Torrey (ATL), Walter Gordy, Rev. David Livingston (Stanley NC), James Cunningham, and Pastor Andre Jennings. John Hudson was an extraordinary friend that encouraged me to write for many years. I genuinely miss him. I will honor him through his widow Toni. Special thanks to Ron Carter, who gave me my first big break contracting with the City of Charlotte Neighborhood development.

My special nieces are Shenise Burton, Sherry Adams Stevenson, Nephew-Gary Stevenson, and my special nephew William O. Hull and Parks D. Durham. And two extraordinary people in David Farmer and Stevie Glenn who went away too soon. Four cousins make having a family awesome: Leonard Watson, Lee Conner, Darryl Barber, and Rev. Darryl Jackson of

St. John Missionary Baptist. Tim L. Penn of Concord, NC, is a man of character. The best neighbors you can ask for are Mr. & Mrs. Reggie & Harvey Rivers and Daughter Sidney, Ian & Michelle Carnejos, Sherrod Coates, and his wife Jennifer, makes a community and super parents. Best friends for Life Fredrick (Bay) Hill and Tony Hill. Finally, my first cousin, Perry Glenn.

Please do not confuse The Master Managers Handbook as a religious text; it is a book about understanding your Faith. It provides revelation knowledge of removing the Yoke of bondage Religion brings in today's cult-like world following political sways and self-serving commercial ministries and organizations. It introduces you to the true freedom of a living Faith (Word) of a core belief system, God's original intention for man's relationship with Him and the Holy Spirit.

Proper understanding and knowledge empower you with enlightenment. However, true refinement of clarity comes only through a higher existence, in my Faith, God's Holy Spirit. I have identified five laws that complete our journey to enlightenment. God has outfitted you with everything you need in life to govern your existence.

Special thanks to Tonya P. Barber, Patrick E. Barber II and Khalil Cliette.

THE MASTER MANAGERS HANDBOOK

- ## A SIMPLE FAITH

- ## SINGLENESS OF PURPOSE

- ## CONFLICT RESOLUTION

- ## EASY BUT POWERFUL

- ## MIND TRAFFIC

- ## CORE BELIELF SYSTEM

- ## TIME ASSIGNMENTS

- ## SELF GOVERNANCE LAWS

- ## MIND FUSION

BENEFITS

*Learn the power of a Core Belief System and how it can change your life.

*Inspiration and knowledge that addresses real life situations.

*Learn the secret to living your "best life" in today's world.

*Gain a simple faith that actually works.

*Learn how to make decisions "right now".

*Gain access to the powerful "Mind Traffic Flow Chart" that shows you how to govern and manage your reactions to all situations.

*Learn how to make time your servant, not the other way around.

*Master your reality by learning how to manage your life in accordance with true nature.

*Learn what "real faith" is, not the cult of religion.

*Experience real power from knowledge and understanding of your position as a Master Manager.

*Better understand personal relationships

*The manual for life and personal coach

*Know who you are and your abilities

*Better understand your purpose in life

*Instant courage to believe in yourself

*Develop goals with confidence

*Better understand the tools you have

Manage your household and have your best life NOW!

TABLE OF CONTENTS

"Now to him (God) who can strengthen you, as promised
in the Good News entrusted to me and in the
Proclamation of Jesus Christ, following the revelation of
that hidden purpose, which in past ages
was kept secret but now has been revealed
(Romans 16:25)."

You cannot go where your mind will not take you.

Patrick E. Barber Sr.

ABOUT THE AUTHOR

I am Patrick E. Barber Sr, born in Gaston County, from a small North Carolina city. I have experienced running multiple Companies, Military, Banking & Finance, Real Estate, Construction, Entertainment, and Record labels during my life. In addition, I participated as a Co-Buyer of an NBA Team and was installed on the Board of multiple Major Corporations as a Director. I have done everything I wanted to do except fulfilling my purpose.

This book is the interrupter of traditional, institutional, religious ideologies and educational philosophies. My ideology and philosophy are an alternative to the ceremonial structures of the pastoral rule. Amazingly, everyone is searching for the secret to life. There is no secret; there is only understanding and truth. Common sense should rule here.

My biggest inspirations were my mom, dad, Napoleon Hill (Think and Grow Rich), Les Brown's inspirational and motivational speaking. That also included W. Clement Stone (Believe and Achieve), Andrew Carnegie (Gospel of Wealth), Og Mandino (The Greatest Miracle in The World). Jim Rohn (My Philosophy for Successful Living), Zig Ziglar (Goals), Tony Robbins (with many credits to his name), and the most important was the Bible.

Following these great teachers was like going deep into the jungle and as I walked. While walking, dropping breadcrumbs to find my way back out, only to realize later animals had eaten the crumbs as I walked deeper and deeper. I soon understood they all had a positive influence in different ways; each seemed to draw from the same Well. They had their slight differences but the same perspective—all great in their way.

What was missing was the knowledge of understanding. I get the PMA, but I could not keep it because it was not my own. It takes more than hype to change and transform your mindset for an accelerated change with the power to change your life from within, forever. You were born with the tools, but rarely do we know how to identify or use them. Most have no idea they exist. You will learn from "The Master Managers Handbook" where those tools are and how to use them. You have unlimited power and a source of energy, and it is yours to keep, I Promise. Trust me.

Today I see millions of people affected by all these diagnoses of mental illness. I know it's just MIND TRAFFIC. The lack of understanding of our minds creates a backlog of congestion that I call mental debris. This causes us to act out in all kinds of ways because the mind is powerful and active. It must be entertained; without a system of interpretation to decipher this information driven by the energy, you can become delusional because it needs a place to go. This can only happen when you harness the powers of Universal, Natural, Spiritual, Success, and Personal Laws. These are the tools to fill the voids we have suffered. Many have almost got it right but, I have it right.

I've watched the most extraordinary individuals implode due to the misunderstanding of mental flow. The five laws must be active to control all aspects of your life. Instead, they spiral out of control, trying to control. Every thought and idea must be captured and held. Nothing must be allowed to "just to be released." Unfortunately, many of these people have no reset or mind triggers.

These are just a few people operating with uncontrolled mind traffic.

- Britney Spears
- Kanye West
- Mike Tyson
- Tiger woods
- Bill Cosby
- Bill Gates
- Elon Musk
- Naomi Osaka
- Chrissy Teigen
- Demi Lovato
- Steve Young

- Donny Osborne
- Michael Phelps
- Dan Reynolds
- Leonardo DiCaprio
- Daniel Radcliffe
- Lady Gaga
- ADELE
- Michael Jackson
- PRINCE
- Kim Kardashian
- Cam Newton

I've had to deal with it all. Still, it wasn't until I decided to live according to the five laws and a core belief system that I anchored to that automatically created my boundaries, from which I gained an understanding and the actual knowledge of "Mind Traffic," which is everything.

When I understood who and what I was, it was easy to decide my every action because of my foundational truths. Recently I was asked what Church I attended; without hesitation, I responded that I take my Church everywhere I go because I am the Temple. Everything I need comes from the inside, and everything outside is an external condition that is controllable.

NOTHING IN THIS BOOK WORKS WITHOUT UNDERSTANDING FORGIVENESS OF ANY AND ALL, INCLUDING YOURSELF. FORGIVENESS IS NOT FOR THE OFFENDER; IT IS TO FREE YOURSELF FROM RELINQUISHING CONTROL TO EXTERNAL FORCES.

FREE YOURSELF FROM THE ENTANGLEMENTS OF PRIDE AND EGOTISTICAL BEHAVIOR

Romans 6:4

King James Version

4 Therefore, we are buried with him by baptism into death: like Christ was raised from the dead by the Father's glory, even so, we also should walk in newness of life.

"A new mindset accelerated change."

PREFACE
BORN WITHOUT A MANUAL

I wish I would have known this truth 51 years ago when I first accepted Jesus Christ as Lord and Savior. I feel robbed of all the benefits I could have had. If only I had known the "whole truth" about engaging the Spirit without religious, church doctrine. Only one fact was sound to this date, Jesus Christ is a personal savior. God did not intend for us to guess our way through life. But, for sure, God is real, and all power is in Jesus Christ, who is alive in us. The Holy Spirit is in us and is our teacher. Our lives here are brief, and I don't want to spend it all on reading instead of being led by the Spirit.

Without God, there is no hope; this is what I believe. Following convictions by emotions is not Faith. It is in the knowledge of your Faith in action that is the source of all power. When this truth is understood, your waiting on God is over; he becomes alive and active in you. God himself is your strength because he is already present within you if you truly understand him. Matthew 7:7, God said to ask, and gives it to you; seek, and you will find; knock, and it will open the door to you. Everyone who asks receives and seeks finds, and to him who knocks, the door will open. 2 Corinth 1:20 His promises are yes, and amen. But John 14 confirms everything about our relationship with him.

Believe it or not, you are already in the mansion. You do not know it yet. When Jesus was on the cross and said, "it is finished," it was finished. All power was in his hands, and he gave this power to you through the crucifixion. We should live by foundational truths provided by our core belief system. With a proper understanding and knowledge of what we truly believe, we have a purpose. Still, it is your responsibility to seek it out, which comes through being led by the Spirit, and you will become hungry for knowledge. A seed in an apple has its DNA to multiply and produce after its kind; its information, "preloaded," from the inception of creation; no one must tell it to become an apple. So, are we?

The creator has given navigational tools to every human alive today and critical laws for every life event. These laws are external and cannot be changed, so we must learn to adapt because they are the pathways and the keys to a more productive life. They will develop your core belief system and accelerate immediate responses to any situation. What you believe is the anchor to your truth, and your core belief system is your choice to accept. I will not and cannot judge you; it is a decision you must make.

"In all things seek understanding."

(Proverbs 4:7, The beginning of wisdom is this: Get insight. Though it cost all you have, get understanding.)

"Take every thought into captivity." 2 Corinthians 10:4-6 and be stewards over everything he had made.

The Church is supposed to be a spiritual leader.

Many churches have failed to meet people's spiritual needs because they lack the Spirit's interaction with the carnal man. The shifting sands may provide some grounding for some of us, but others are hopeful for a world that engages a compromise of God's Word to entertain the world and its dying society. Some of us wonder if there is a safe place to be vulnerable. Some of us want to develop the empathy that supports a call to action and justice, while others have no desire for compassion nor want any justice except for their purpose, and it is ever-shifting to suit their needs. In their view, they're neither right nor wrong, simply their way.

The people of this world are experiencing unbeknownst challenges with no hope or understanding of how God would allow such actions to occur. First off, God did not create or allow any of this mess; it's all man's own doing. He gave the management of this world to the man on the day Adam received his instructions. Man has been in charge ever since, and chaos has ensued ever since. If that was not true, why do Presidents call themselves commander in chief? Why do news reporters all over the world call the President the most powerful man in the world?

Why do countries led by dictators call themselves superpowers, desiring just as Lucifer desired to be God? Each is wanting the title of the most formidable President on Earth or the most powerful nation. We are living in a world that no longer turns to the Church as a guide. And many of those who are turning to the Church as a guide is now mortally wounded in this world system. The great falling away has occurred because the Church has sorted out its authority under the government by its entanglements with governments. They want to agree with Pontius Pilate; instead of God's rule, the government should have no power over the Church.

Just as Jesus stood at the point of death in front of Pontius Pilate, he stated, you have no power over me except for what my Father in heaven gives you. Do you not think that he would not send twelve legions of Angels if I called my Father to protect me? Matthew 26:53

The alternative messages and misinformation concerning the Holy Spirit have weakened the people of God, whereby they have no protection or power from the Holy Spirit. Many testify they were speaking in tongues to confirm the Spirit; what about the other Gifts that come with the Holy Spirit and his power to speak blessings and healing over situations?

While I was writing my book, I was trading significant volumes of Cryptocurrencies; the market knocked out over half of my investment, in some cases as much as seventy-five percent. But I had an initial reaction; I just said wow and continued to write. At that time, about 90% of my income was coming from trading. So, I told my wife we were income locked, and when I finish the book, God will restore my original investment, and he will supply our needs in the meantime. He provided more than I was making, and on the last day of writing my book, my initial investment was back in my account. I told her the rest of the world would benefit from it.

Right standing and understanding the Spirit is all I needed to navigate through these times. Just as I was losing my sight, that has also been restore. I only stand in expectancy of the promise.

I look forward to our voyage together toward being what God truly intended for the true power of his people.

I know who God is; God is a collective of one. Therefore, when a believer believes, you will find him—the SECRET of one.

Romans 8:9

You, however, are not in the flesh but the Spirit if the Spirit of God dwells in you. Therefore, anyone who does not have the Spirit of Christ does not belong to him.

"The greatest DETOX a person can do is FORGIVE."

Reset Daily

CHAPTER 1

THE ASSIGNMENT OF THE MASTER

From the beginning of Adam and Eve to now, it has been just over 6000 years. Also, it has been 2000 years since Jesus Christ, according to the scripture, mainstream religious leaders, bible scholars, and bibles in the United States. According to the first book of the Bible, we see God started his creation of the world and completed it with Adam, then Eve, then he rested.

It does not matter from my perspective whether it was Six Thousand years or Six Million years; according to my philosophy (Faith), regardless, we all still must believe in something. But it is a personal choice and your decision. Freewill is the power of acting without the constraint of necessity or fate, the ability to operate at one's discretion.

The Bible said God instructed Adam to follow his command not to eat a specific tree. This creation event is what I accepted and adopted as my core belief system. Genesis 2:2 says, On the 7th day, God ended all the work he had made and rested from all his labor. I emphasize ALL his work. The truth is when it is all said and done, God created Adam and gave him a job. Genesis 2:15, the LORD God put the man to work and take care of the Garden of Eden. As we see here, God is a creator, not a manager. According to King James, Adam fails his first commandment he instructed him not to do. Of all things, he had absolute power and authority over except one thing: the tree of knowledge, which was off-limits.

Eve was not around when God instructed him, yet he blamed God for giving him the woman. And God said to Eve, because you have done this thing, for this reason, Adam should rule over you. (Gen 3:16) "Even though accepted as fact, remember we are following a belief system we accept according to our spiritual walk, interpretation, and acceptance." Depending on the doctrines you follow, the Christian Bible states it as a fact, but there is no private interpretation. (2 Peter 1:19-21)

Adam and Eve were deceived in the garden by partaking from the one tree God instructed them not to eat. And the story states they realized they were naked when they had consumed the fruit. So, God cursed the serpent and scorn Adam and Eve by opening the current conditions and removing them from the garden; additionally, their actions caused sickness, disease, and death for all humans.

The reality is that Eve was the mother of abortions through her sin against God. But why did God allow these actions? God has always had the power of judgment. The more significant question is what God meant. What did he say about our roles in our daily decisions? Better yet, what do you believe? God gave Adam one command to keep the long and short of it, nothing like the Ten commandments. Adam was told not to eat of the tree of knowledge. Thus, he fails his only assignment.

God is the all-powerful creator, and now we must seek why God, in all his strength, would allow his creation to violate his covenant with man. Why would another creature he created

2

have contention with members of his creation? In everything that God created, Eve was God's last creation.

There is no discrepancy in God's plan, only in man's understanding of it. People form opinions of any religion or belief that is different from theirs. I have one view, and that is what I believe. Let God be the judge of someone else's heart. Everyone thinks that their Faith is the only truth and the only way, and they should. But I have no right to condemn anyone. (Roman 14) With so many religions and conflicting doctrines, it is overwhelming and confusing. God has gifted us with a spirit of power, love, and sound mind, not fear. It all leaves you wondering why God asks Adam where he was after he disobeyed his command when he is all-knowing.

Further, why did his creations know they were naked, discerned they failed, and the serpent was also his creation whose primary goal was to deceive. If we accept this belief system of design, we must also follow the Word he stated in all things to seek understanding as an absolute. ["Most people don't THINK."]

Knowledge is the perceived idea of acceptance of your truth. You must know why and what you believe and have absolute confidence and power over the decisions you make. It is hard to define true purpose unless you can anchor to a core belief system. If left unanswered, your life is baseless on false claims and far worse, powerless. God's Word is absolute and brings power and makes you free from bondage. The law of Moses is 613 commands, Jesus Christ fulfills them all.

The wonderful part of God's plan is straightforward, but man complicates with religion. I have never read the Word of God say thou must be Baptist; thou must be Catholic, Jew or Gentile. Instead, I have seen throughout the accepted text I believe, Man cannot please God without faith, and thou must have Faith. "I believe the best demonstration of Faith is going from failure to failure with no loss of enthusiasm."

I am a Christian, But I am not religious, nor do I follow a religion; I follow Faith, trust God, and receive his Son, Jesus. With the traditional religious institutions, your Faith is on an algorithm. Zigzagging, up and down, never stabilized and stuck on an emotional roller coaster. (Isaiah 26:3 Those who trust in thee will be kept in perfect peace, for they are keeping their minds on God.) **("Jesus said because you don't know the Scriptures or the power of God, you're deceived." — Matthew 22:29)**

This is life under the law without mercy and grace.

My Faith is constant and never changes, just as in God's Word. If you received Jesus, you received God. (John 10:30 my Father and I are One) (Eph 4:5 There is one Lord, one Faith, one baptism.) But the [a]Helper (Comforter, Advocate, Intercessor — Counselor, Strengthener, Standby), the Holy Spirit, whom the Father will send in My name [in My place, to represent Me and act on My behalf], He will teach you all things. And He will help you remember everything that I have told you (John 14). It has become a commercial business for guilt and shame. Still, with my simple, as a child-like approach,

4

(Matt 18:3 "Truly I tell you," He said, "unless you change and become like little children, you will never enter the kingdom of heaven.) Thus, I am free from the bondage of sacred rituals that enslave personal commitments to a particular group, sector, or culture.

Jesus Christ is my Point of Beginning; "All power is given unto me over Heaven and Earth." (Matt 28:18)

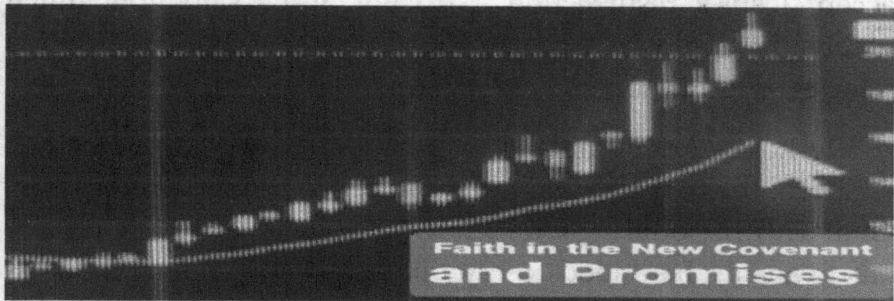

Faith in the New Covenant and Promises

The Truth Will Make You Free

31 So Jesus said to the Jews who had believed him, "If you abide in my word, you are truly my disciples, 32 and you will know the truth, and the truth will make you free." 33 They answered him, "We are offspring of Abraham and have never been slaves to anyone. How is it that you say, 'You will become free?'"

34 Jesus answered them, "Truly, truly, I say to you, everyone who practices sin is a slave to sin. 35 The slave does not remain in the house forever; the Son remains forever. 36 So if the Son makes you free, you will be free indeed. 37 I know that you are offspring of Abraham, yet you seek to kill me because my Word finds no place in you. 38 I speak of what I have seen with my Father, and you do what you have heard from your Father."

5

You must take the time to know who you are. What you believe, the feeling is deeply rooted in your actions, regardless of how you got here, the question you must ask is, now what? My answer is simple. I accept my truth, and it is my core belief system. There is nothing God has to prove to me.

I trust him as the creator and believe in His promises and the covenant. Thomas needed to touch his wounds before he would accept Jesus's resurrection. I do not. Jesus said how much greater it would be if you could believe without seeing his injuries, without touching his wounds. (John 20:29)

We know Adam and Eve's story and how they conceived children, the first two being Cain and Abel. How Abel pleased God with his offerings, and how Cain was jealous and slew Abel causing his blood to cry out from the ground. Gen. 4:8 "And Cain talked with Abel, his brother: and it came to pass when they were in the field, that an argument came up against Abel, his brother, and slew him." Afterward, Cain left his native country, traveled to another country, and took a wife (Married). Not to point out inconsistencies, but to establish an acceptance of the incident as inspired by God, or whether it is.

Gen 4:17 *"And Cain knew his wife, and she conceived, and bare Enoch: and he built a city, and called the name of the city, after the name of his son, Enoch."*

Here is yet another major conflict if you were looking for controversy. It does not matter to me because I do not know anybody that can confirm or deny what happened, except for Jesus coming. After all, he is the only relevant conversation. When they deny the Holy Spirit its full authority, it is an excuse for the powerlessness of today's ministers.

I proposed where she came from and how they got there since Adam and Eve were the first creations. Cain traveled to another land and took a wife; who was she and her people? So many ask these questions, and still no good answers. These things are not issues for me because I have accepted the truth of who God is to me.

Jesus then gave up his Spirit after crying out again with a loud voice. From top to bottom, the Temple curtain parted at that moment. In a flash, rocks split, the earth shook, and tombs burst. It is said that many saints who had died returned to life. They went out of the graves after Jesus' resurrection, went into the holy city, and appeared to many people.

Matthew 27:50-53

He certainly is God, and His Son Jesus was born of the virgin Mary, crucified, and rose again, in my opinion. I have no more of a historical record than any theologian. Therefore, I decided to accept this as my discipline and core belief system, and anchor. Archaeologists can fabricate any evidence and time zones they want; no one knows for sure; it all goes back to belief. I do not personally know any Greek scholars of the Biblical past. It is all that you will accept and believe. We give the status to men of the cloth as a high priest as though they directly connect to God, and you do not.

To me, God's plan is simple. The Yoke and bondage of traditional religious groups create boundaries of a commercialized community, and talking heads building loyalty to a particular group or sect. It is almost cult-like following a political Party's point of view. My allegiance is to Jesus Christ and taking ownership of the promises delegated by his authority from the creation in the garden approach.

Let us look at God's intent in creating man and the directive given to humanity through Adam.

My perspective is not a theory, and it is my belief and my opinion, just as any other writer of biblical ideas and interpretations. Uninspired doctrine by men does not inspire me, presented by men born in the flesh. There are over 4200 religions throughout the world. "I believe," let God be true, and every man a liar. (Romans 3:4 "God forbid: yea, let God be true, but every man a liar; That thou might be justified in thy sayings, and might overcome when thou art judged." King James Version (KJV))

What makes me think I know the answers to the many questions? My answer is I do not know all the answers. Nobody has all the answers or proof of anything; it is all that you are willing to believe. The Just shall live by Faith. In my opinion, you must think before you consider anything as fact. I am not religious; I am a Christian that lives by Faith. I do not need God to keep proving himself to me because I have already accepted the facts of Jesus. Can any of you prove me wrong? Just as Jesus said, I am not seeking glory for myself. My teaching is to help fulfill the blessing of your Faith to have life and more abundantly.

The hardest part of a core belief system is self-awareness: To convince yourself you can be more than you are. Acceptance of philosophy and ideologies is challenging because of our stubbornness and rebellious nature. Learning to trust yourself is more complicated than trusting someone else. Trust me; we have minimal time to live on this Earth. I would rather live my days with peace of mind and a solid footing to build my foundation. Life should not be so hard. Matt 11:30, *"My Yoke is easy and my burden light."*

8

If you follow someone else and fail, your selfish nature feels right to blame someone else. Comfort and conformity are the worst that you can ever allow in your mind for self-development. In my core belief system, the center is Jesus Christ. Even though there are over 4200 different religions and some, I choose Christianity. I accept what I follow. Every individual has a right to believe whatever they want, and it is your choice. I follow what I feel, just like the By-laws and governance of a corporation. I think that "anyone" who serves any faith, religion, or God, better knows Jesus, in my opinion.

The by-laws are self-governance and the truth of understanding a perceived knowledge of what I believe, and nothing else matters. In the end, it is all about my feelings and a transparent understanding that creates balance in your Faith which empowers your spiritual guidance and knowledge.

You are in charge with a clear mandate from your Faith; you are free to accept his promises regarding the covenants of agreements you take as your truths. With this authority given by God, you can receive all that you can believe. (James 2:17 Thus, Faith by itself, if it does not have works, is dead.) We say we trust God but do nothing on our own; God has rested already in his labor.

Genesis 2:2-3 KJV

2. And on the seventh day, God ended his work which he had made, and he rested on the seventh day from all his work which he had made.

3. God blessed the seventh day and sanctified it because he had rested from all his work that God created and made.

We expect God to be a laborer for our needs when he has given us his promises and the power of the "word," which is tangible and more physical than Gold. But it is just too simple to believe. But that is precisely the way it is. God is not a manager; He is a Creator. When God created Adam, he finished all his work, sat Adam down, and gave him his job description and scope of work.

Gen 2: 15, *The Lord God took the man and put him in the Garden of Eden to work it and take care of it. 16 And the Lord God commanded the man, "You are free to eat from any tree in the garden; 17 but you must not eat from the tree of the knowledge of good and evil, for when you eat, from it you will certainly die."*

ANOTHER INTERPRETATION:

Gen 2:15 And the Lord God took the man and put him in the Garden of Eden to tend and guard and keep it. Gen 2:17 But of the tree of the knowledge of good and evil and blessing and calamity you shall not eat, for in the day that you eat of it you shall surely die. He did not die immediately; he now would die in the flesh. (Died at the age of 930 years) Now because of Adam and Eve, we all will die. Before they took off the tree, there was no sickness or death.

What happened inside the Garden was Adams's responsibility from the beginning; God gave him authority to make decisions over his entire creation.

Gen 1:26, *And God said, "let us make man in our image, after our likeness: and let them have dominion over the fish of the sea, and over the fowl of the air, and the cattle, and the Earth, and over every creeping thing that creepeth upon the Earth."*

10

27 So God created man in his image, in God's image created; male and female created them.

28 And God blessed them, and God said unto them be fruitful, multiply, replenish it, and subdue it: and have dominion over the fish of the sea, and over the fowl of the air every living thing that moved upon the Earth.

29 And God said, Behold, I have given you every herb bearing seed, which is upon the face of all the planet, and every tree, in the which is the fruit of a tree yielding seed; to you, it shall be for meat.

30 Every beast of the Earth, every fowl of the air, and to every thing that creepeth upon the Earth, wherein is life, I have given every green herb for meat: and it was so. (See the Story of the Lion).

31 And God saw Everything that he had made, and behold, was excellent. And the evening and the morning were the sixth days.

"Trust in the Lord with all thine heart and lean not to your own understanding. In all thy ways acknowledge him, and he shall direct thy paths."

(Proverbs 3: 5-6)

11

CHAPTER 2

THE MASTER MANAGER

What is a Master Manager? The name came from the beginning when God created Adam and Eve; God told him To manage the garden, multiply and be fruitful, and be stewards over everything he had made, to go and subdue the Earth. We are to rule over every beast of the land, fish in the sea, and fowl of the air. When God created Adam, He made him in His likeness and image and instructed him to make choices whenever he decrees. Adam and Eve broke the relationship and sinned against God by choosing to eat the fruit, resulting in sin's corruptible nature. God sent his Son to restore the damage and offered him as a sacrifice from himself. When Jesus, crucified, died and was buried, he rose in power and with the gift of the Holy Spirit. God never rescinded the free will of man. So, Jesus said whosoever turns from sin will be saved (repent), and God would send the Holy Spirit in his place. He will take up residence in you through the Comforter. After this takes place, you would receive power Galatians 3:29 says, "There is neither Jew nor Greek, there is neither bond nor free, there is neither male nor female": We are All God's people.

Jews vs. Gentiles

Religion, culture, and other aspects of Jewish and gentile traditions are different: Jews are descendants of the patriarch Israel. Thus, Jehovah was worshiped by Gentiles according to the patriarchal system. Although the Jews worshiped God according to the law of Moses, the Gentiles relied on Jesus as their Savior.

Judaism celebrates their belief in being descendants from God but does not respect Gentiles. Although it has been agreed that God initially made Adam and Eve

In Latin, gentiles mean belonging to a tribe or clan. The term gentiles refer to non-Israelite tribes in the King James Version of the Bible. But today, Gentile stands for "non-Jew." The word "Jews" is from Hebrew Yehudim.

Gentiles are considered non-Hebrew people who were descendants of Abraham of Israel. On the other hand, the Jewish patriarchs of Abraham, Isaac, and Jacob are all traced to the same ancestry.

Jewish belief teaches that the Messiah will descend from heaven and unite all under God's Kingdom; they do not consider Jesus the Christ the awaited Messiah.

They think that this Messiah will bring justice and peace to everyone through the unification of humanity. But, on the other hand, the gentiles believe in every other thing that the Jews believe. In modern times, Christians are called gentiles, and as such, they believe in the Son of God.

Jews follow Judaism, and Gentiles follow Christianity. Judaism is decentralized, and there is no one like the Pope or other decision-making authorities as in Christianity. Each

Jewish congregation is separate, headed by a spiritual leader call a Rabbi.

Main Point:

But in the Master Managers, we only care about what God said to Jesus in addition to what Jesus says to us through the Holy Spirit. Through Faith, you must be clear on what you believe, why you think it, and what you will do about it. The focus here is to get you to shake up the Spirit in you. Everyone has a spirit, and it is up to you to accept a belief system. Everyone on the planet has one, even if they will not admit it. Even an atheist believes in nothing.

To me, what you choose to believe in is on you. My belief is in Faith, and it all started with Jesus; I do not and will not dilute my Faith in Christ's risen event dealing with all the chaos from the beginning of creation. I believe God said, let God be true and every man a lie because he knows all and the thousands of religions globally, and the fact is everyone thinks they are right.

Romans 3:4

God forbid yea, let God be true, but every man a liar; as written, that thou mightest be justified in thy sayings, and mightest overcome when thou art judged.

This book is not religious; it is a book about the power you have and how to unleash it, whether you are a believer in my faith or not. Although, your belief in a God or higher intelligence has a bearing on your acceptance of a particular idea. Still, for the most part, you will reap the same benefits of success as anyone else using the philosophy and ideologies.

"Let the dead bury the dead" why did he say this? The most misunderstood perception of God's Word is when I go to a

14

funeral and hear the people grieving, saying that we will see you again and believe it. Yet, most have no belief system other than what they heard in Church, through friends or family. But they suffer in every other part of their life, living paycheck to paycheck, defeated lifestyles.

Still, they believe they will see this person supernaturally in the afterlife. If that is an accurate statement, then this person should have been born again in the Spirit, with the Spirit alive in them. But if they can genuinely believe this as a fact, how come Jesus's impartation is not acceptable but taught in churches worldwide? Again, a form of Godliness, but they deny the power thereof.

Most believers do not accept the fact that Jesus says I am in you. He clearly stated that I am going away to come back and live within you "physically," and you will receive power when I return. Their lack of knowledge is the reason they are living without the real power of the Spirit. All the things Jesus said he would do, he did.

We are empowered to do these things and are supposed to be able to do them as well. But unfortunately, countless people have died that could have been saved by the power of God. But because they only accepted the Spirit in Word and not in the physical, many have perished prematurely, and others cannot live their best life right now. Death is something we will all see, but it should not be our focus; living should.

Many religious institutions teach this weak watered-down doctrine to avoid the responsibility to deliver the gifts of the Spirit because many do not possess them themselves. "But suppose they can believe in this miracle," then why can't they believe in the things that make them happy and healthy? Something they need to live with, just as a lovely home, money,

15

cars, and fine food? God's promises are for believers. God tells us to have faith in him; there is no other prerequisite and limits to what you can have. The Comforter which will come in his name will teach you.

Only you can believe for yourself. God only gave Adam a few instructions to follow. He gave them also to you — millions of books written and most excluding the actual truth. The Bible has the laws of Moses and commandments, and Jesus the great commandment whereby he fulfills the law. The writers wrote and built this wall of confusion, and with our narrow vision, we stop seeking. God didn't stop inspiring his_Word with only a few. Do you think God is silent with the Bible written by millions of religious scholars, diluting his authority in a man?

That's why Jesus said, "Let the dead bury the dead"; they have no life. Without truth, you are dead to life. I am not trying to make you stop believing in God; I am trying to show you the wisdom and power of God. God is a yes God; his promises are yea and amen. Why? Because I accept it as so. Whatever I take and decide to believe are the by-laws of my beliefs, and they create the boundaries and drives me to my purpose. The idea that they will see their deceased love again is a form of Godliness, but they deny the power to live without genuine Faith.

Even my Faith states when it rains on the righteous, it also rains on un-righteous alike. See the story of the wheat and the tares.

Matthew 13:24-30

The Parable of the Wheat and the Tares

24 Another parable He put forth to them, saying: "The kingdom of heaven is like a man who sowed good seed in his field; 25 but while men slept, his enemy came and sowed tares among the wheat and went his way. 26 But when the grain had sprouted and produced a crop, then the tares also appeared. 27 So the owner's servants came and said to him, 'Sir, did you not sow good seed in your field? How then does it have tares?' 28 He said to them, 'An enemy has done this.' The servants said to him, 'Do you want us then to go and gather them up?' 29 But he said, 'No, lest while you gather up the tares, you also uproot the wheat with them. 30 Let both grow until the harvest, and at the time of harvest, I will say to the reapers," First gather together the tares and bind them in bundles to burn them but gather the wheat into my barn."""

But it states, others were casting out demons in the name of Jesus; they were confused about how the others who were not in their discipleship could do such miracles.

And John answered him, saying, Master, we saw one casting out devils in thy name, and he followeth not us: and we forbad him because he followeth not us. But Jesus said, Forbid him not: for there is no man which shall do a miracle in my name, that can lightly speak evil of me. For he that is not against us is on our part. (Mark 9:38-40)

It is all about your belief in what you possess.

17

"Because of Your Unbelief"

I. If it stands God's will to heal and Jesus healed this boy (Matt. 17:18), why could not the disciples heal him?

  A. The disciples who asked Jesus this question, "Why could we not cast him out?" They thought that it was God's will to heal.

  B. They had already been given power and authority to heal the sick and cast out devils. (Matt. 10:1 and 8).

  C. Hence the disciples were confused.

  D. The answer Jesus gave in the first part of Matthew 17:20 is very revealing:
Because of your unbelief.
Matthew 17:20

  E. This is simple, but it is profound.

II. Every instance where Jesus ministered healing, Faith was involved.

  A. Some people may argue, "What about in Luke 7:11-16 where Jesus raised the boy from the dead in the city of Nain?"

  B. It was Faith for this widowed mother to allow Jesus to interrupt the funeral procession and her grief.

  C. If Faith were not present, she and the others there would have reacted very differently.

III. We just saw that if we were to ask the average person, "Why isn't everyone healed," most people would answer, "Well, it's because they don't have enough faith."

A. It is true that if a person is not operating in Faith, it will hinder them from receiving, but that is not what the Lord said.

B. He said it was because they had unbelief.

IV. Certain versions of the Bible render Matthew 17:20 inaccurately, saying, "Because you have so little faith."

A. If you were to look at many of the translations, especially the more literal ones, this verse is rendered "Because of your unbelief," not "Because you have so little faith."

B. Most people have this concept that if they believe God, that automatically means they do not have any unbelief.

C. This is not what the Word teaches:
For verily I say unto you, whosoever shall say unto this mountain, Be thou
removed, and be thou cast into the sea; and shall not doubt in his heart, but
shall believe that those things which he saith shall come to pass; he shall have
whatsoever he saith.
Mark 11:23

D. If being in Faith truly meant you automatically had zero unbelief, why did Jesus include the part about not doubting in your heart?

E. The truth is, you can believe and disbelieve at the same time.

V. Consider the parallel passage of this Father and his demonized boy in Mark 9-

And they brought him unto him: and when he saw him, straightway the
Spirit tares him, and he fell on the ground and wallowed foaming. And
he asked his Father, how long is it ago since this came unto him? And he
said, Of a child. And ofttimes it hath cast him into the fire, and into the
waters, to destroy him: but if thou canst do anything, have compassion
on us and help us, Jesus said to them if thou canst believe, all things
are possible to him that believeth.
Mark 9:20-23

A. Now look at how this Father responded:
   And straightway the father of the child cried out and said with tears,
   Lord, I believe; help thou, my unbelief.
   Mark 9:24

B. The Lord did not correct him, rebuke him, or say anything like that; He just cured the boy.

C. This shows that you can have faith and unbelief at the same time.

D. Imagine a team of horses hooked up to a wagon. Under normal circumstances, they would have enough power to move that wagon. But, if you had a group of horses, was equally hooked to the other side of the wagon and, both teams were pulling simultaneously in the opposite direction, the net effect would be zero.

E. This is what Jesus was saying in the first part of Matthew 17:20.

F. He didn't tell His disciples, "It's because you don't have enough faith"; He said, "It's because of your unbelief. Your unbelief canceled out the Faith you had."

VI. Translating this "Because you have so little faith" makes no sense when you look at the rest of Matthew 17:20:

> For verily I say unto you if ye have faith as a grain of mustard seed,
> ye shall say unto this mountain, Remove hence to yonder place, and it
> shall remove, and nothing shall be impossible unto you.
> God Wants You Well

A. Jesus was saying, "If your faith is only the size of a mustard seed, nothing would be impossible to you."

B. You do not need immense Faith; you need a faith that does not cancel out, counterbalance or negate by unbelief, pulling in the opposite direction.

CHAPTER 3

GOD'S SPECIAL IMPARTATION OF HIS SPIRIT

When God said, let us create them in his image, it was not like the human form you and I imagine; it is the Holy Spirit within a unique presence in a relationship. Nothing in the Bible clearly states whether Adam did or did not have the Holy Spirit. However, the first chapter of Genesis describes that God created humankind, namely Adam and Eve, in His image, and 2 Corinthians 3:18 states that what makes a man be in God's image is the Holy Spirit.

Genesis 1:1-3

21st Century King James Version

1 In the beginning, God created heaven and the Earth.

2 And the Earth was without form and void, and darkness was upon the face of the deep. And the Spirit of God moved upon the face of the waters.

In Genesis 6:3, when God decides that the Holy Spirit will not stay forever in the man; This reveals to us that the Holy Spirit indwelt in man after their fall in sin.

So, the Lord said, *"My Spirit will not remain with human beings forever, because they're truly mortal. Their lifespan will be 120 years."* (Genesis 6:3)

On the other hand, in Genesis 2, God warns Adam that the day he will eat from the tree of knowledge of good and evil, he will undoubtedly die. However, the day he ate from the forbidden tree, Adam did not die immediately. Instead, that day he died spiritually (he lost the Holy Spirit) as we find it written in Paul's epistle to Ephesians: Adam lived 930 years of age according to Genesis 5:5.

You who were dead because of your offenses and sins that you once practiced, as you lived according to the ways of this present world and according to the ruler of the power of the air. This is the Spirit that is now active in those who are disobedient. Indeed, all of us once behaved like them in the lusts of our flesh, fulfilling the desires of our flesh and senses. By nature, we were destined for wrath, just like everyone else. But God, who is rich in mercy, because of his great love for us even when we were dead because of our offenses, made us alive together with the Messiah (by grace you have been saved), raised us with him, and seated us with him in the heavenly realm in the Messiah Jesus. (Ephesians 2: 1-6)

The takeaway is the Master Managers Handbook is a book about believing, having faith in what you think. We all believe in something, but what do we believe? What you believe can thrust you to greatness or make you homeless. Everybody believes in something right or wrong; it's a matter of "what do you believe." Many of us claim we have Faith; it doesn't matter in who or what, but a Faith in something that consumes and gives nothing in return is a complete waste of all your resources, time, money, and energy.

Faith is what allows you to stand when all others falter. Faith is not always associated with religion, but in most instances, it is. People follow cults, religion, family traditions, and politics, which seems to have become the new religion, bordering on witchcraft. I'm making the point that you must decide why you believe in something that affects every facet of your life. When you have a core belief system, there is no drifting. You have chosen to follow your conviction, nothing can change or move you from it, and when turbulence comes, you are always centered and able to stand.

When I understood Faith for myself, and as I grew in the Word of God, I anchored my Faith in Jesus Christ. Some believe in Jesus's name, some that believe in Jesus and the Holy Spirit, and some that he sent the Comforter, which is the Holy Spirit, and he lives inside you, but rarely that he is alive in you. Most teach it, preach on it, speak about having it, even tongues, but deny the power of its presence, and your Faith is your choice. I am not here to argue or judge you over who's religion is correct since there are over 4200 plus religions and some 30,000 plus practicing some forms of religions, not to mention the hundreds of different bibles, even a slave bible, and many interpretations and the commercialization of the Church.

IF YOU ADD ALL THE CONFLICTING STORIES AND ASSUMPTIONS, YOUR HEAD WILL SPIN. None of these is something I even consider because of my point of beginning. From the age of nine, I wanted to please God. For over 50 years, God has always been on my conscience. It took me the last 20 years to fully understand the state of religion and the role man has played in interrupting God's plan for our individual lives. As I began to understand, I also stood in what I believed, and God did just what he promised. Unfortunately, I wasted most of my life trying to fit into a mold of someone else's making—the deception of religion.

I realize we don't live 900 years, and I don't have 400 years like in Egypt to be in slavery waiting on the Lord to return; what I know now changed it all because of all the unanswered questions. I had many questions and no answers, and I felt as delusional as so many others who stray from the path because they become detached to cope. My Faith now is straightforward, direct, and accessible without all the religious baggage, and my religion is Faith, as he stated in Matthew 11:30, that his Yoke is easy. Religion is the bondage of a cult when misused and misunderstood. I have no denomination to call my own. My Faith is in Jesus Christ and Him alone. It's your decision what foundational truths you will allow governing your life. So many believers are already left behind because they misunderstood his Word.

I believe the Comforter shall teach me and lead me to all understanding, and it does. But it only happened after I understood how to engage the Spirit of God and accept the Words, and they are the Bread and Water of the physical interpretation. Each Word is Life itself, and they are the assets of everything we say and do, and it all becomes tangible. So please make no mistake about it until I understood four things; I had no real victories in my life.

- **One: The "Word" is physical and has life.**

- **Two: He lives inside just as when you drink water, it goes inside.**

- **Three: Take every "word" into captivity, Take them, prisoner.**

- **Four: Forgive everyone, even if they do not deserve it. (Reset and Delete Mental Debris)**

"If you do not empty the trash bin in your computer or do maintenance, it will run sluggish."

Your life must be run just like a business; make no mistake about it. You are "your name," CEO. You are fully equipped with everything to be successful. You are the hardware and software, and you now have a system. But suppose you do not know how to cope with this external system. In that case, you will suffer just as a data breach, and indeed suffer a malware attack and find yourself unproductive because of the mental debris that are the viruses of this society. There is enough conflict in every religion, and I don't have a religion; I have a Faith. My beginning point is in Jesus Christ, and as you read the book, you will know why. All the scriptural references in this book are the words of confirmation of the Word alive in YOU.

I don't subscribe to all the historical baggage since, in my Faith, Jesus is the Gate, and there is no other way to enter. No one enters except through Christ. Imagine having the Faith of a straight line and not an algorithm of up and down. Life can and is simple. When we were born, most of us have the same inventory as the next person; understanding how to use them is the difference. When we have 24 hours, five senses, six faculties, and understand the value of "Time Assignment," we find substitutes for what is missing or doesn't have.

You have under your management 86,400 seconds in a day. Use them wisely and make them your laborer instead of existing in time. This is your life; live it; only God knows what comes next. I know of no one except Jesus, as my Faith can validate what is right and wrong, and that is because I have chosen to believe him. Jesus said that" All Authority" is given to him over heaven and earth. Therefore, I don't need interpreters with the Holy Spirit living inside me when He is my teacher. Our belief is to choose a faith and live by our convictions; no one knows except the Spirit.

MERCY AND GRACE

Let us look at what the dictionary says about Grace and Mercy: An act of grace is characterized by courteous goodwill. The gift is neither asked for nor deserved but given freely. By contrast, mercy is the act of compassion and kindness toward someone in your power to punish or harm. The goal is to ease someone's suffering.

Ephesians 1

21st Century King James Version

1. Paul, an apostle of Jesus Christ by the will of God, To the saints who are at Ephesus, and to the faithful in Christ Jesus: 2. Grace be to you and peace from God our Father and the Lord Jesus Christ. 3. Blessed be the God and Father of our Lord Jesus Christ, who hath blessed us with all spiritual blessings in heavenly places in Christ, even as 4. He hath chosen us in Him before the foundation of the world, that we should be holy and without blame before Him in love, 5. having predestined us to be His own adopted children by Jesus Christ, according to the good pleasure of His will, 6. to the praise of the glory of His grace, wherein He hath made us accepted in His Beloved:

7. in Whom we have redemption through His blood, the forgiveness of sins, according to the riches of His Grace, 8. wherein He hath abounded toward us in all wisdom and prudence. 9. He hath made known unto us the mystery of His will, according to His good pleasure which He hath purposed in Himself,

10. In the dispensation of the fullness of times, He might gather in one all things in Christ, both which are in heaven, and which are on Earth, even in Him. 11. In Christ also we have obtained an inheritance, being predestined according to the purpose of Him who worketh all things after the counsel of His own will, 12. that we, who first trusted in Christ, should be to the praise of His glory. 13. In Christ ye also trusted after ye heard the word of truth, the Gospel of your salvation, in Whom also after ye believed, ye were sealed with that Holy Spirit of promise, (Ephesians 1:1-13)

Besides, Genesis 5 specifies that Adam and Eve have been created in the image and likeness of God, but after his fall, Adam gave birth to a son in his image and likeness, not in the image of God. It happened

because Adam lost the embodiment of creation the very second he fell into sin. This image we can regain by being born again. He did not realize he was even naked before they sinned and was only exposed after he sinned. He had no understanding of this beforehand.

This is the historical record of Adam's generations. When God created humankind, he made them in His likeness. Creating them male and female, he blessed them and called them humans when he created them. After Adam had lived 130 years, he fathered a son just like him, that is, according to his likeness, and named him Seth. (Genesis 5:1-3)

GOD GAVE US A SECOND TREE

Adam and Eve were never supposed to know evil, but their disobedience caused God to act and re-establish a new relationship with Jesus the Vine, and we are the branches. (John 15: 1-17)

"Malachi 3:6, For I am the Lord, I change not; therefore, ye sons of Jacob are also not destroyed." (What God promised he promised, and you can expect whatever you believe according to your Faith)

So, the fall of man forces God to push the reset button with Noah and his family. Now, belief systems and religions rapidly flow. The misrepresentations, confusion, and ideas of the events after the Ark had landed on dry land have spun all types of conclusions. The primary discrepancy is no real explanation for the multiple races worldwide. I could fill a book with unlimited interpretations.

With all the social media, dating apps, and adult sites, promoting all types of perversion on the Internet, porn apps, etc., it leaves me wondering why our current society, which probably dwarfs their sin in comparison, is spared. Could it be that man does not understand what God is saying or misunderstand how to interact with God?

This is the corrective action by God to send His Son Jesus and where the mystery starts. It all parallels with Adam and his failure in the garden, in my opinion. First, God communicated to the prophets than the prophets to man, and then God sent Jesus, post-crucifixion the comforter to man. A simple plan.

John 15

New International Version
The Vine and the Branches

15 *"I am the true vine, and my Father is the gardener. 2 He cuts off every branch in me that bears no fruit, while every branch that does bear fruit, he prunes so that it will be even more fruitful. 3 You are already clean because of the Word I have spoken to you. 4 Remain in me, as I also remain in you. No branch can bear fruit by itself; it must remain in the vine. Neither can you bear fruit unless you remain in me?*

5 *"I am the vine; you are the branches. If you remain in me and I in you, you will bear much fruit; apart from me, you can do nothing. 6 If you do not remain in me, you are like a branch that is thrown away and withers; such branches are picked up, thrown into the fire, and burned. 7 If you remain in me and my words remain in you, ask whatever you wish, and it will be done for you. 8 This is to my Father's glory that you bear much fruit, showing yourselves to be my disciples.*

9 *"As the Father has loved me, so have I loved you. So now remain in my love. 10 If you keep my commands, you will remain in my love, just as I have kept my Father's commands and remain in his love. 11 I have told you this so that my joy may be in you and that your joy may be complete. 12 My command is this: Love each other as I have loved you. 13 Greater love have no one than this: to lay down one's life for one's friends.*

14 *You are my friends if you do what I command. 15 I no longer call you servants because a servant does not know his master's business. Instead, I have called you friends, for I have made known to you Everything that I learned from my*

Father. 16 You did not choose me, but I chose you and appointed you so that you might go and bear fruit—fruit that will last—and so that whatever you ask in my name the Father will give you. 17 This is my command: Love each other.

I would instead teach the truth of the Faith walk that I understand than spend my time being mysterious engaging mystical elements of the Universe when God is a straight and narrow path. God has no secrets withheld from his people. Whatever you choose to believe in, believe it whole heartily at least, you will get results. When it rains on the Just, it also rains on the Unjust. If you sow a seed, you will reap the harvest. It does not matter what you sow; it yields a return to the Sower.

Cornerstones of your Faith.

1. **God Is I AM**

2. **Jesus was Crucified and is Risen**

3. **New Covenant is in Jesus as High Priest**

4. **God's law and Promises Fulfilled in Jesus**

5. **God's Will is for Man to know Jesus and Recieve the Comforter**

These are the five pillars for which the core belief system stands.

They are the anchors to the truth of my core belief system because God cannot lie or change; he is immutable.

(Num. 23:19; 1 Sam. 15:29; Ps. 102:26; Mal. 3:6; 2 Tim. 2:13; Heb. 6:17–18; Jam. 1:17)

1 Timothy 2:4, KJV: "Who will have all men to be saved, and to come unto the knowledge of the truth."

Romans 7:12— "The law is holy, and the commandment holy, and just, and good" (also Romans 7:14).

Romans 8:28–30

28 And we know that all things work together for good to those who love God, to those who are the called according to His purpose. 29 For whom He foreknew, He also predestined to be conformed to the image of His Son, that He might be the firstborn among many brethren. 30 Moreover whom He predestined, these He also called; whom He called, these He also justified; and whom He justified, these He also glorified.

The New King James Version (NKJV)

CHAPTER 4

WE SHOULD LIVE BY FAITH

Jesus Christ's birth is the single defining moment — rather than from the very beginning of creation.

"Jesus coming was the fulfilling of the law of Moses."

Matthew 15

DEFILEMENT COMES FROM WITHIN

1 Then, the scribes and Pharisees from Jerusalem came to Jesus, saying, 2 "Why do Your disciples transgress the tradition of the elders? For they do not wash their hands when they eat bread."

3 He answered and said to them, "Why do you also transgress the commandment of God because of your tradition? 4 For God commanded, saying, 'Honor your father and your mother'; and 'He who curses father or mother, put him to death.' 5 But you say, 'Whoever says to his father or mother," Whatever profit you might have received from me is a gift to God" — 6 then he need not honor his father or mother.' Thus, you have made the commandment of God of no effect by your tradition. 7 Hypocrites! Well did Isaiah prophesy about you, saying:

8 *'These people draw near to Me with their mouth,*

And honor Me with their lips,

But their heart is far from Me.

9 *And in vain they worship Me,*

Teaching as doctrines the commandments of men.'

10 *When He had called the multitude to Himself, He said to them, "Hear and understand: 11Not what goes into the mouth defiles a man; but what comes out of the mouth, this defiles a man."*

12 *Then His disciples came and said to Him, "Do you know that the Pharisees were offended when they heard this saying?"*

13 *But He answered and said, "Every plant which My heavenly Father has not planted will be rooted up. 14 Let them alone. They are blind leaders of the blind. And if the blind leads the blind, both will fall into a ditch."*

15 *Then Peter answered and said to Him, "Explain this parable to us."*

16 *So Jesus said, "Are you also still without understanding? 17 Do you not yet understand that whatever enters the mouth goes into the stomach and is eliminated? 18 But those things that proceed out of the mouth come from the heart and defile a man. 19 For out of the heart proceed evil thoughts, murders, adulteries, fornications, thefts, false witness, blasphemies. 20 These are the things which defile a man, but to eat with unwashed hands does not defile a man."*

A Gentile Shows Her Faith.

21 Then Jesus went out from there and departed to the region of Tyre and Sidon. 22 And behold, a woman of Canaan came from that region and cried out to Him, saying, "Have mercy on me, O Lord, Son of David! My daughter is severely demon-possessed."

23 But He answered her not a word.

And His disciples came and urged Him, saying, "Send her away, for she cries out after us."

24 But He answered and said, "I am not sent but unto the lost sheep of the house of Israel."

25 Then she came and worshiped Him, saying, "Lord, help me!"

26 But He answered and said, "It is not good to take the children's bread and throw it to the little dogs."

27 And she said, "Yes, Lord, yet even the little dogs eat the crumbs which fall from their masters' table."

28 Then Jesus answered and said to her, "O woman, great is your Faith! Let it be to you as you desire." And her daughter received healing that very hour.

Jesus Heals Great Multitudes

29 Jesus departed from there, and came nigh to the Sea of Galilee, went up on the mountain, and sat down there. 30 Then great multitudes came to Him, having the lame, blind, mute, maimed, and many others; and they laid them down at Jesus' feet, and He healed them. 31 So the multitude marveled when they saw the mute speaking, the maimed made whole, the lame walking, and the blind seeing, and they glorified the God of Israel.

Feeding the Four Thousand

32 Now Jesus called His disciples to Himself and said, "I have compassion on the multitude because they have now continued with Me three days and have nothing to eat. And I do not want to send them away hungry, lest they faint on the way."

33 Then His disciples said to Him, "Where could we get enough bread in the wilderness to fill such a great multitude?"

34 Jesus said to them, "How many loaves do you have?"

And they said, "Seven, and a few little fish."

35 So He commanded the multitude to sit down on the ground. 36 And He took the seven loaves and the fish and gave thanks, broke them and gave them to His disciples; and the disciples gave to the multitude. 37 So they all ate and were filled, and they took up seven large baskets full of the fragments that were left. 38 Now those who ate were four thousand men, besides women and children. 39 And He sent away the multitude, got into the boat, and came to the region of Magdala.

FAITH IS THE ONLY TRUTH
GOD DOES NOT CALL US TO LIVE BY RELIGION BUT FAITH.

The birth of Jesus Christ is the essential single defining moment—rather than from the beginning of creation. Your freedom begins here. We go out of our way to learn something that does not benefit us at all. The most important lesson you will ever learn is communicating from within with the Spirit that lives within you. Acceptance of his existence internally is the beginning of unlimited possibilities in receiving whatever you ask by Faith. Most ministers stay away from this one thing because it forces them to act, and most do not have the Spirit supercharged.

Matthew 15:6-9

Jesus explains it well. They are not to honor their father or mother with it. Thus you nullify the word of God for the sake of your tradition. These people honor me with their lips, but their hearts are far from me. They worship me in vain; their teachings are merely human rules.

John 3:3

Nicodemus asks the question; Jesus replied, "Very truly I tell you, no one can see the Kingdom of God unless they born again. 4: How can someone be born again when they are old? 5: And Jesus answered him and said unless you are born of water and the Spirit. (which is the Comforter.) 6: Flesh gives birth to Flesh. Spirit gives birth to Spirit. 7: Jesus said you should not be surprised. 8: The wind blows wherever it pleases. You hear the sound, but you cannot tell where it comes from or where it's going. So is everyone born with the Spirit. (Jesus said you people desire a sign, but your belief is the conduit to everything not seen)

Ephesians 5:18

And do not get drunk with wine, for that is debauchery, but be filled with the Spirit.

Acts 2:4.

And they were all filled with the Holy Spirit and began to speak in other tongues as the Spirit gave them utterance.

Acts 4:31

After they prayed, the place they gathered shook, all filled with the Holy Spirit, and they continued to speak the Word of God with boldness.

Acts 1:8.

"But you will receive power when the Holy Spirit has come upon you, and you will be my witnesses in Jerusalem and all Judea and Samaria, and to the end of the earth."

Luke 11:13

"If you then, who are evil, know how to give good gifts to your children, how much more will the heavenly Father give the Holy Spirit to those who ask him!"

1 Corinthians 12:13

For in one Spirit, we were all baptized into one body—Jews or Greeks, slaves or free—and all were made to drink of one Spirit.

1 Corinthians 6:19

Or do you not know that your body is a temple of the Holy Spirit within you, whom you have from God? Therefore, you are not your own.

1 John 1:9

If we confess our sins, he is faithful and righteous to forgive us our sins and cleanse us from all unrighteousness.

1 Thessalonians 5:19

Do not quench the Spirit.

2 Corinthians 3:17

Now the Lord is the Spirit, and where the Spirit of the Lord is, there is freedom.

Acts 11:24

For he was a good man, full of the Holy Spirit and Faith. And a great many came to Christ, were added to the Lord.

Acts 13:52

And the disciples were filled with joy and with the Holy Spirit.

Acts 13:9.

But Saul, also called Paul, filled with the Holy Spirit, looked intently at him.

Acts 2:38

And Peter said to them, "Repent and be baptized every one of you in the name of Jesus Christ for the forgiveness of your sins, and you will receive the gift of the Holy Spirit."

Acts 4:8.

Then Peter, filled with the Holy Spirit, said to them, "Rulers of the people and elders."

Acts 6:3.

Therefore, brothers, pick out from among you seven men of good repute, full of the Spirit and wisdom we will appoint to this duty.

Acts 7:55

But he, full of the Holy Spirit, gazed into heaven and saw the glory of God and Jesus standing at the right hand of God.

Acts 9:17

So, Ananias departed and entered the house. And laying his hands on him, he said, "Brother Saul, the Lord Jesus who appeared to you on the road by which you came has sent me so that you may regain your sight and receive the Holy Spirit."

Ephesians 4:30

And do not grieve the Holy Spirit of God, by whom sealed you for the day of redemption.

Galatians 5:16

But I say, walk by the Spirit, and you will not gratify the desires of the flesh.

Galatians 5:22

But the fruit of the Spirit is love, joy, peace, patience, kindness, goodness, faithfulness.

Hebrews 9:14

How much more will the blood of Christ, who through the eternal Spirit offered himself without blemish to God, purify our conscience from dead works to serve the living God.

Isaiah 44:3

"For I will pour water on the thirsty land, and streams on the dry ground; I will pour my Spirit upon your offspring, and my blessing on your descendants."

John 1:33

I did not know him, but he who sent me to baptize with water said to me, "He on whom you see the Spirit descend and remain, this is he who baptizes with the Holy Spirit."

John 14:16

"And I will ask the Father, and he will give you another Helper, to be with you forever."

John 14:17

"Even the Spirit of truth, whom the world cannot receive because it neither sees him nor knows him. You know him, for he dwells with you and will be in you."

John 14:26

"But the Helper, the Holy Spirit, whom the Father will send in my name, he will teach you all things and bring to your remembrance all that I have said to you."

John 15:26

"But when the Helper comes, whom I will send to you from the Father, the Spirit of truth, who proceeds from the Father, he will bear witness about me."

John 6:63

"It is the Spirit who gives life; the flesh is no help at all. So, therefore, the words that I have spoken to you are Spirit and life."

Luke 1:15

For before the Lord, he will be great. And he must not drink wine or strong drink, and he will receive the Holy Spirit, even from his mother's womb.

Luke 1:41

And when Elizabeth heard the greeting of Mary, the baby leaped in her womb. And Elizabeth was filled with the Holy Spirit.

Luke 1:67

And Zechariah was filled with the Holy Spirit and prophesied, saying.

Luke 24:49

"And behold, I am sending the promise of my Father upon you. But stay in the city until you have the power from on high."

Mark 1:8

I have baptized you with water, but he will baptize you with the Holy Spirit.

Matthew 28:19

Go all nations and make disciples baptizing them in the name of the Father and of the Son and the Holy Spirit."

Matthew 3:11

I baptize you with water for repentance, but he who is coming after me is mightier than I, whose sandals I am not worthy to carry. Therefore, he will baptize you with the Holy Spirit and fire.

Romans 15:13

May the God of hope fill you with all joy and peace in believing so that by the power of the Holy Spirit, you may abound in hope.

Romans 8:14

For all who the Spirit of God leads are sons of God.

Romans 8:26

Likewise, the Spirit helps us in our weaknesses. For we do not know what to pray for as we ought, but the Spirit himself intercedes for us with groanings too deep for words.

Romans 8:9

You, however, are not in the flesh but the Spirit if the Spirit of God dwells in you. Therefore, anyone who does not have the Spirit of Christ does not belong to him.

It saddens me when I hear ministers preaching funerals and speaking of how the angels picked another flower and taken them home to heaven as if everyone goes to be with the Lord. They may have never confessed salvation, but Ministers must speak the truth. It is the religion that makes it very hard to accept the Holy Spirit living inside by Faith because of their lack of knowledge, understanding, and denying the power of God.

CHAPTER 5

WE ARE ALREADY IN THE MANSION
(HE THAT HAS EARS TO HEAR WHAT THE
SPIRIT IS SAYING)

2 Samuel 9

David asked, "Is there anyone still left of the house of Saul to whom I can show kindness for Jonathan's sake?"

Now there was a servant of Saul's household named Ziba. So, they called him to appear before David, and the king said to him, "Are you Ziba?" "Your servant," he replied.

The king asked, "Is there no one still left of the house of Saul to whom I can show God's kindness?" Ziba answered the king, "There is still a son of Jonathan; he is lame in both feet. (crippled)

"Where is he?" the king asked. Ziba answered, "He is at the house of Makir, son of Ammiel in Lo Debar."

So, King David had him brought from Lo Debar from the house of Makir, son of Ammiel.

When Mephibosheth, Son of Jonathan, the Son of Saul, came to David, he bowed down to pay him honor. David said, "Mephibosheth!" "Your servant," he replied.

"Don't be afraid," David said to him, "for I will surely show you kindness for the sake of your Father, Jonathan. I will restore to you all the land that belonged to your grandfather Saul, and you will always eat at my table."

Mephibosheth bowed down and said, "What is your servant, that you should notice a dead dog like me?"

Then the king summoned Ziba, Saul's servant, and said to him, "I have given your master's grandson Everything that belonged to Saul and his family.

You and your sons and your servants farm the land for him and bring in the crops to provide for your master's grandson. And Mephibosheth, grandson of your master, will always eat at my table." (Now Ziba had fifteen sons and twenty servants.)

Then Ziba said to the king, "Your servant will do whatever my lord the king commands his servant to do." So, Mephibosheth ate at David's table like one of the king's sons.

Mephibosheth had a young son named Mica, and all the members of Ziba's household were servants of Mephibosheth.

And Mephibosheth lived in Jerusalem because he always ate at the king's table, and he was disabled (CRIPPLED) on both feet.

Why is this story relevant to you? Is it straightforward? When Adam and Eve took the fruit, the relationship was destroyed. Jesus was crucified on the cross. When he walked out of the tomb, the Holy Spirit was made available to all that repented, and upon doing so, the Holy Spirit took up residence inside. Wherever Jesus is, you are. It may be hard to understand, and it is never taught in this way, but you are already in the Kingdom, in Jesus. There is only One Father, One

Son, and One Holy Spirit. If he lives in you, what happens? God himself came into you because they are one. The comforter will come back to you in Jesus's place, the Holy Spirit. Another mystery is why God would judge himself; he wouldn't? This is also a truth; we have bypassed this judgment in Jesus. The blind has led for so long they believe their lack of knowledge to be true.

"I WILL GO AWAY AND RECEIVE YOU UNTO MYSELF"

God sent his Son Jesus to die on the cross from the Kingdom of Heaven to reconcile the blending of spirit and Flesh. This is where every Christian of every faith seems to lack knowledge and belief. They had vacated the power of God for what Jesus did for you and me, being God himself in the form of sinful Flesh to redeem us from the garden of Eden. For whatever reason, the man refuses to accept his rightful place in the powerful position that he restored in the relationship. God does not have a relationship with Flesh; he has it with Spirit because the Flesh is corruptible. The breakdown is in the false teachers failing to perform the miracles of Jesus. They have no power. Plain and simple.

1 Thessalonians 5:23 KJV

And the very God of peace sanctify you wholly; I pray God your whole spirit and soul and body be preserved blameless unto the coming of our Lord Jesus Christ.

There is only One God, One Son, and One Holy Spirit. Jesus stated I must go away; if I do not, you cannot receive the gift of the Holy Spirit. He constantly says my Father and I are one. He said I would come back to you and receive you unto myself. This is the whole truth of power in the following:

John 14
King James Bible
Jesus Comforts the Disciples

1. Let not your heart be troubled: ye believe in God, also believe in me.

2. There are many mansions in my father's house: I would have told you if it were not so. I go to prepare a place for you.

3. If I go and prepare a place for you, I will come again, and receive you unto myself; that where I am, there ye may also be.

4. And whither I go ye know, and the way ye know.

5. The Way, the Truth, and the Life

6. Thomas saith unto him, Lord, we know not whither thou goest; and how can we know the way?

7. Jesus saith unto him, I am the way, the truth, and the life: no man cometh unto the Father, but by me.

8. If ye had known me, ye should have known my Father also: and from henceforth ye know him and have seen him.

9. Philip saith unto him, Lord, shew us the Father, and it sufficeth us. 9. Jesus saith unto him, Have I been so long time with you, and yet hast thou not known me, Philip? He that hath seen me hath seen the Father; and how sayest thou then, Shew us the Father?

10. Believest thou not that I am in the father and the father in me? I speak not of myself the words that I say unto you: but the Father that dwelleth in me, he doeth the works.

11. Believe me that I am in the father, and the father in me: or else believe me for the very works' sake.

12. Verily, verily, I say unto you, He that believeth on me, the works that I do shall he also do; and greater works than these shall he do because I go unto my Father.

13. And whatsoever ye shall ask in my name, that will I do, that the Father may be glorified in the Son.

14. If ye shall ask anything in my name, I will do it.
Jesus Promises the Holy Spirit
(Joel 2:28-32; John 16:5-16; Acts 2:1-13; Acts 10:44-48; Acts 19:1-7)

15. If ye love me, keep my commandments.

16. And I will pray for the Father, and he shall give you another Comforter, that he may abide with you forever.

17. Even the Spirit of truth; whom the world cannot receive, because it seeth him not, neither knoweth him: but ye know him; for he dwelleth with you and shall be in you.

18. I will not leave you comfortless: I will come to you.

19. Yet a little while, and the world seeth me no more; but ye see me: because I live, ye shall live also.

20. At that day ye shall know that I am in my father, and ye in me, and I in you.

21. He that hath my commandments, and keepeth them, is he that loveth me: and he that loveth me shall be loved of my Father, and I will love him and will manifest myself to him.

22. Judas saith unto him, not Iscariot, Lord, how is it that thou wilt manifests thyself unto us, not the world?

23. Jesus answered and said unto him, if a man loves me, he will keep my words: and my Father will love him, and we will come unto him, and make our abode with him.

24. He that loveth me not keepeth not my sayings: the word ye hear is not mine, but the Father's which sent me.

25. These things have I spoken unto you, being yet present with you.

26. But the Comforter, which is the Holy Ghost, whom the Father will send in my name, he shall teach you all things, and bring all things to your remembrance, whatsoever I have said unto you.

   Peace I Leave with You
   (Romans 5:1-5)
   King James Bible

27. Peace I leave with you, my peace I give unto you: not as the world giveth, give I unto you. Let not your heart be troubled, neither let it be afraid.

28. Ye have heard how I said unto you, I go away, and come again unto you. If ye loved me, ye would rejoice, because I said, I go unto the Father: for my father is more significant than I.

29. And now I have told you before it comes to pass that ye might believe when it is come to pass.

30. Hereafter, I will not talk much with you: for the prince of this world cometh and hath nothing in me.

31. But that the world may know that I love the Father; and as the father gave me commandment, even so, I do. Arise, let us go

We have the mind of Christ and all the things associated with the Holy Spirit.

FSH=FATHER SON AND THE HOLY SPIRIT:

The Trinity is a threefold concept that tells us that God exists as three persons, all co-eternal and consubstantial, the Father, the Son, and the Holy Spirit (derived from Latin word triad = trinus).

MBS= MIND, BODY, AND SPIRIT:

God has expressed that our wellness is not just Spiritual but Mental and Physical, all working together to get a fruitful and balanced life. Our Mind coexists with our Will, our Body houses the Soul, and our Spirit coexists with God. (Comforter)

CARNAL SPIRIT=MIND, BODY, AND SOUL:

The Carnal man consists of the Mind, which coexists with the Will. The Body is the housing and the physical of the man, and the Soul, whereby it is the Carnal. To be Carnal, is to live by the desires of the flesh, self-absorbed. This person has excluded God from their life and does not know Jesus personally.

***All faculties operate out of the Mind. ***

We are master managers, and we manage everything. Our health, wealth, and spirituality. Anything associated with us or our interests. We walk in expectancy because we walk by Faith. Miracles happen in mind first; if you can believe it, you can achieve it and receive it. God put Adam in the garden to manage and work. Because Adam had a body, he needed to be physical. God knew what Adam would need before he made him. But he also knew it was Adam's decision over all that he had made. God looks for obedience and faith; they are synonymous with each other. God can do anything he wants, but why would he create Adam and do all the work? Adam and Eve were the models of the coming generations, but they fail to keep God's command. For you to walk, you must stand first.

We are no different from any other fruit or vegetable from a garden. The body is the same; It requires food, water, nutrients, vitamins, and minerals because we are Earth. The sooner we understand our duties to the body, the better we are. We are the living billboards of life. We are temples, and we house the Holy

Spirit. Therefore, it would be best always to strive to look your best, just as the temple is adorned with beauty. This is not a costly array.

This is about seeing the value in yourself and a certain mindset with Spiritual authority over your Mind, Body, and Soul. You are the manager who manages your body; if it needs a doctor go, God has provided them for you; if you cut your finger off, it's not going to grow back; let them reattach it. I've heard, "well, Jesus put the soldier's ear back on," great. But a doctor can help with this as well; it is one that Jesus will provide.

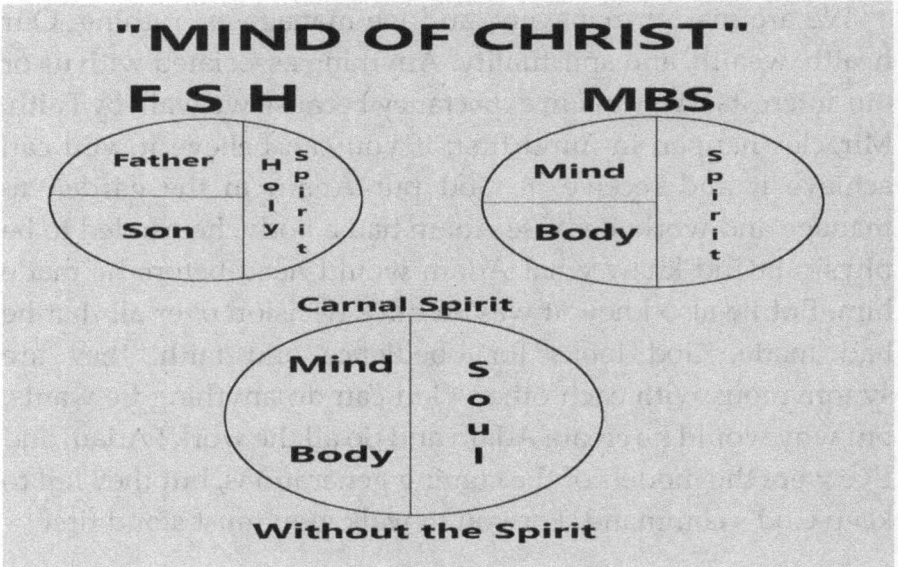

WHAT ARE CORE BELIEFS.

YOU HAVE TO BELIEVE TO BELIEVE

Core beliefs are fundamental beliefs about our mindset and how we engage our faith and other people; Deep down, beneath all our "surface" thoughts, they are things we believe to be absolute truth. Essentially, core beliefs determine how you perceive and interpret the world.

Our heart is the warehouse of our subconscious mind, and the subconscious mind is the library of the conscious mind; they both act as a fulfillment center for desires and needs. It establishes backlinks to fulfill the information you have stored, accepted, and approved, and your Ego awaits an opportunity to administer. When something happens, your Ego will open the subconscious mind and consult the core belief that is most likely to defend you against any offender that violates your rules.

Core beliefs are the conviction of the heart. A core belief is something you accept as truth without question. That means you can expect every day it will seem just as valid as it was the day before. When beliefs become conviction, your mind lives in a free flow state without fears and doubts of making an irrational decision. This is done without thinking about them, questioning them, or even being aware of them because the boundaries of your beliefs determine your actions.

Defining your core belief system is imperative because it helps you Identify your degree of worthiness, safety, competence, power, and love. Positive thinking leads to a healthy sense of self-worth and self-acceptance. Your core beliefs significantly influence your sense of belonging and the primary picture of how others view and treat you. Our mind works by pictures that it sees and forms.

You are the artist and creator of the world you see. When the image starts, the subconscious mind receives the image, starts, creates, and builds the vision.

It works as an additional hard drive of a computer add-on, a slave drive. It sends backlinks to be bridged to complete pathways until it is clear of your desired results. So, it does not stop until it reaches a solution or resolves. It fully intends to complete the picture—that is why we focus on what we want. You are sure to get it through your internal network through your higher intelligence. (In my faith, higher intelligence is God)

The subconscious mind is an open door, and it does not reject anything. Whatever you release from your conscious mind goes into the subconscious mind. Therefore, leaving anything you do not want out is crucial and accepting only your desired results. Before anything enters your mind, you must take every thought into captivity, so everything must be scrubbed and filtered for malware and viruses, creating mental debris. Most of your time will be to reset or master the art of delete. Forgiveness is the master delete button to have a fresh, clean start without negative anchors or drama every day.

Your beliefs dictate the rules you follow. These beliefs are formed in us at an early age by our environment, culture, DNA, thoughts, experiences, the things we see other people do, and the advice others give us while growing up.

The ability to manage this is understanding the physical and mental tools you already have will help fight against influences that can hinder your efforts to succeed. Politics, Religion, and Economics dominate; it only takes one to control all three. But a core belief system frees you from being led by either and gives you enlightenment and power to self-rule within your mindset.

The noises and chatter that come from the outside early in life confuse us because we cannot identify within ourselves the power to interpret the things of life. Parents, teachers, and friends teach us and interacting with friends, etc. From all the misinformation, mental debris is created and not managed; this becomes the minefields of the mind.

When we are a Pre-teen, we are thoroughly confused. After all, we do not know what to do because we do not understand how to identify ourselves. There is nothing wrong with not understanding what you do not know or know because you have no philosophy or share in a different ideology. These are values and skills parents should teach if they only knew.

The problem is most of us do not have a clue until now. We, as humans, do not think about all the things a trusted party exposes to us. We should be aware that this failure to think about things given to us as facts are not always as they appear. Common sense would win most of the time.

This attitude toward accepting historical facts is baffling. Higher powers at work give us insight and understanding that provide us with more excellent knowledge and self-awareness. For example, scientists use the legend of time loosely as 150,000,000 years, a billion years, really. Like, Caveman between 10000 and 40000 years ago. SMH. (Shaking my head) Why should we care now. There remains absolutely nothing to learn from them. We are not attempting to rebirth a dinosaur.

But according to Biblical text, Adam and Eve were just over 6000 years ago, and Jesus over 2000 years ago. Using today's records, you can find four ancient civilizations in the world, including China. More than 3,000 years ago, China's written history began during the Shang Dynasty (1700-1046 BC)... It makes it easy to follow Jesus because he is the reference point for all nations regardless of religion.

The simple fact is hardly anyone understands this knowledge of the universe. It has laws that complement the discipline of a core belief system. Belief systems stem from the roots of ancestral generations, attitudes, environments, culture, race, religion, politics, and economics. The Master Manager's Handbook removes the excuses of barriers placed by the generational curses of politics, beliefs, race, and economics. Specifically, anything that happens before Jesus. You become the force of change.

Understanding the fullness of a core belief system's internal mindset will directly impact how you perceive the world and interpret what happens around you to formulate the rules you live by daily. For this reason, negative core beliefs can have a massive effect on our self-acceptance, self-worth, and self-esteem. Therefore, block all negative influences, no exceptions.

When you appropriately access the philosophy and ideology of the Master Managers Handbook, you empower your affirmations with accelerated change. But, unfortunately, most of us live on surface thoughts because nothing else exists. We seek external motivation from motivational speakers, and life coaches to help keep us excited about a venture or keep the positive energy flowing. But, still, it does not last because it is not accurate or a part of you.

In the master manager's handbook, our philosophy is simply rejecting what you do not want and accept what you do. Your core beliefs are the very foundation of all actions. Five laws govern everything: They dictate what you will and can become; they are your rules. Therefore, is it so crucial to self-talk and have the first meeting of the day with yourself?

Take a little time with your mind. When you ultimately establish the fullness of your core belief system, it becomes an automatic filter that interprets life's daily challenges and situations. There is no doubt that it is a self-fulfilling prophecy. With proper instructions, your world becomes "your world." It becomes what you make it to be.

YOUR WORLD IS FULL OF LUST AND PRIDE

Lust is the most toxic and dangerous emotional stimuli; it is the EGO's best self-preservation tool for selfish inhibitions. It does not consider empathy or emotional pain. It is a pure chemical of sex on the brain. Lust is a destructive nature driven by endorphins, a physical and mental drug. Crack cocaine does not register on a scale compared to lust. Yet, it is responsible for wrecking more lives than any drug on the planet. What is ironic, the justice system and psychologists seem to know its dangers by treating and registering sex offenders when the whole world is on the same network. People are so full of lust and pride they lose a sense of value in people.

Hollywood was the perfect example of a lack of respect for their spouse or partners; now, it seems that the entire world has been affected by years of this type of behavior, and exposure eases its tentacles into society without morals creating a world without a conscience. It is not Hollywood's fault that we fall into this trap; it is the very nature we were born with but never taught how to control it. The bible has answered this question for us. It all starts with the thought, which is where it all begins. Unfortunately, the "Thought" is such a powerful mechanism it suggests that we take every "Thought" into captivity. Lock them down in every sequence of thinking.

Men and women alike destroy their marriages and homes over lust; pride of life makes them act out into a world full of illusions and falsehoods. Yet, the couple will be attached to a society based on the norms of a failed moral system, excluding children, a byproduct of the marriage—just a piece of the puzzle you threw away with no remorse. The psychological damage to the children was never considered. And these events take place to show a status of a Billionaire Businessman, Superstar Athlete, or Entertainer that ages in time to become frail and sick. You are leaving a trail of carnage and ruin, a path of destruction. In the end, your children model you and become copies of past sins.

Your children, growing up in a world full of confusion, having no way to interpret because you have no idea how to contain the same lust that got you there. Well, it all begins with "Thought" and Self Control through a core belief system to create the boundaries needed to prevent a runaway train filled with pride. Of course, understanding who, what, when, and where you are is the key to purpose, but the blending of a core belief system is the better risk to take. The world has existed long enough not to follow ancestral mistakes but adapt to the universe's powers. We lack the knowledge of how to believe, but the fact is you must believe in something, or you will have no hope. That is why suicide happens; people have no hope or lose it.

People need direction, and the mind needs to be amused. This mind is fully functional and on a quest for knowledge and will dock its network to allow inclusion to their comfort. So, it would be best to learn early before getting engaged in relationships what we represent and how we want people to perceive us. Because if it's about you, then you should never marry or have children only to disrupt their lives and make another unhappy human being. Creating a body count on how many people you sleep with is reckless endangerment and irresponsible. Many of these people are married or in relationships with children, and your one-night fling ruins generations' lives.

When you feel the urge to take a flight to the streets for your 20 minutes of pleasure, secret apps on your phone, private email accounts, all these are holes in your soul. Remember I told you that you would wake up to reality in a world of hurt one day and all your making. So be careful what you wish.

UNDERSTANDING IS EVERYTHING, THE KNOWLEDGE TO SEEK IS WISDOM

Wisdom is the principal thing; therefore, get wisdom; Yea, with all thy getting, you must gain understanding. (Proverbs 4:7)

Let us begin by understanding who we are and establish the authority we have been given, in my opinion. First, in my belief, God creates Adam, and then he created Eve. When you break it down, God created Adam and gave him instructions; Eve had not been created when God gave him a job during that time. (The LORD God took the man and put him in the Garden of Eden to work it and take care of it.) Genesis 2:15

The work all begins from the Garden. By the seventh day, God had completed the work that he had done, and he rested on the seventh day from all the work he had done. (Genesis 2:2) And the seal for eternity to all truth; Psalm 33:11 says, "The counsel of the Lord stands forever, the plans of His heart to all generations." His Word is Timeless, and His Promises are Everlasting! In other words, "I am God, and I do not change."

One thing that holds here is he does not change because after Adam's generation failed and God spared Noah's family on the Ark, it seemed that man was at it again in the worst way. And God sent his son Jesus to receive us unto himself through the Holy Spirit (Comforter) because God has intercession with the Spirit of man. "Nevertheless, I tell you the truth; It is expedient for you that I go away: for if I go not away, the Comforter will not come unto you; but if I depart, I will send him unto you." John 16:7.

The flesh is corrupt in every way; that is why he states evil is always present. (Rom 7:21) So, for this reason, we must be born again. Since I serve the living God, that will be Jesus, who is one with God, and the Comforter is the Holy Spirit, and Jesus stated they are one. So, the Holy Spirit is what you must receive to be born again. Without the Holy Spirit, the Spirit of man is carnal and void.

1 Corinthians 15:53-55

For this corruptible must put on incorruption, and this mortal must put on immortality. So, when this corruptible shall have put on incorruption, and this mortal shall have put on immortality, then shall be brought to pass the saying that God said, death is swallowed up in victory.

O death, where is thy sting? O grave, where is thy victory? (1 Corinthians 15:53-55)

To reconcile the union of spirit and flesh from the Kingdom of Heaven

TRUST IN WHAT YOU BELIEVE

Reading the Old Testament seemed to increase my questions concerning it. Not one second do I question the sovereignty of God and the Holy Spirit; God is Absolute and without question God, and God alone, in my opinion. That does not mean I am right and what someone else believes is wrong; they may see things differently and approach the whole concept of belief in their way.

There are over 4200 Religions with over 30,000 different faiths and counting, I do not know what they believe, and I am not the judge of another manservant. But, unfortunately, many Scholars, Teachers, Preachers, Prophets, and Evangelists assume that they have an exclusive contract with God as sole communications directors and translators for the others. I know many of them to have good intentions, and it is what most believe. But they follow a belief they have accepted as all absolute and infallible; there is no such thing with man.

Religion and religious people are dangerous, have very distorted views, are self-centered, and are usually one-sided. I do not care what anyone else thinks because most do not believe what they teach; they follow the crowds and cater to the lust and power of a commercial business rather than empowering the personal experience of a living savior.

It seems to me the whole group missed his last posting of disasters upon humanity. Sadly, many have brought him into politics. God is full of mercy and grace. These disasters facing society have nothing to do with him. By his destructive nature, man is responsible for the carnage we are facing.

Natural disasters are what they are, "Natural." God will separate the wheat from the tares in the end. When it rains on the just, it also rains on the unjust. ("Just" means Righteous)

THE WHEAT AND THE TARES

Matthew 13:24-30
The Parable of the Wheat and the Tares

24 Another parable He put forth to them, saying: "The kingdom of heaven is like a man who sowed good seed in his field; 25 but while men slept, his enemy came and sowed tares among the wheat and went his way. 26 But when the grain had sprouted and produced a crop, then the tares also appeared. 27 So the owner's servants came and said to him, 'Sir, did you not sow good seed in your field? How then does it have tares?' 28 He said to them, 'An enemy has done this.' The servants said to him, 'Do you want us then to go and gather them up?' 29 But he said, 'No, lest while you gather up the tares, you also uproot the wheat with them. 30 Let both grow until the harvest, and at the time of harvest, I will say to the reapers," First gather together the tares and bind them in bundles to burn them but gather the wheat into my barn."'''

Let us ask the hard questions.

Why would God do any of this? He would not, and he did not.

Now let us get to the business of why you are reading this book. Ironically, people like secrets and mysteries; here is a Biggy.

"Great is the mystery of Godliness."

And without controversy, great is the mystery of godliness: God was manifested in the flesh, justified in the Spirit, seen by angels, preached among the Gentiles, believed on in the world, Received up in glory. (Sounds like Jesus to me)

1 Timothy 3:16

They were having a form of godliness but denying the power. And from such people turn away!

2 Timothy 3:5

Who desires all men to be saved and to come unto the knowledge of the truth.

1 Timothy 2:4

The Comforter is the source of my power and my knowledge.

But the Helper (Comforter, Advocate, Intercessor— Counselor, Strengthener, Standby), the Holy Spirit, whom the Father will send in My name [in My place, to represent Me and act on My behalf], He will teach you all things. And He will help you remember everything that I have told you.

John 14: 26

Q. If this is not a religious book, why do I use scriptural references as sources?

A. The answer is simply the fact that Jesus came down from the Father to be a sacrifice for you and me and for anyone willing to accept him as truth. Because he states, Jesus answered, "I am the way and the truth and the life. No one comes to the Father except through me. So Jesus coming was the reset button that changed how we interact with God or your higher intelligence as "High Priest"; he is the "New Covenant."

John 14:6

Jesus made this statement just before he disappeared into the clouds:

7. Jesus replied, "It is not for you to know times or seasons that the Father has fixed by His authority. 8. But you will receive power when the Holy Spirit comes upon you, and you will be My witnesses in Jerusalem, and all Judea and Samaria, and to the ends of the Earth." 9. After He had said this, they watched as he goes up, and a cloud hid Him from their sight. ...

Acts 1: 7-9

Well, Jesus came that we would be free, also that we would not be living in spiritual and religious bondage and life more abundantly. It is clear what he wants for us, but the religious leader seems to have something else in mind. The secrets, the mysterious, magic, and more than anything else, control over your mind and finances.

I am fearless of what man can do to me. If you need proof of this misguided attempt to sway Christians to vote a certain way, look to the 2020 presidential political campaigns using God as a religious tool and telling the American public who God has chosen as president. Nothing could have been further from the truth. Now you know that God does not talk to them.

Republicans and Democrats alike have made their way around the circles of influential religious leaders. These large congregations have considerable power and influence with their followers. Their communities, not God, empower these men and women. Many of these followers follow without questioning the truth or examining the facts; impressive is how they weaponized God's word in hiding it under the cloak of holiness.

"Thou shalt not follow a multitude to do evil: neither shalt thou speaks in a cause to decline after many to wrest judgment" (Exodus 23:2 KJV). Christians say they stand for truth, but they accept all types of hatred and bigotry towards everyone they deem different. Abuse in the Christian community is no different in the secular society. The failure of the churches to recognize the true power of God is the cause of this failure. Powerful politicians' relationships and governmental influence mean more to them than the Power of God. They are operating on surface knowledge and feeling because most do not know the Spirit and power in them, nor can they see it.

It was wrong of the Church and their inability to trust God for putting the fate of the Christian community in such a lukewarm proposition, empowering corrupt men to excise power over the Power of their Faith in politics, as if God needs either Party. Christ told Pontius Pilate that he could not do anything to him except that God allowed it. Jesus had access to legions of angels to protect him. It seems that the church's trust is in Caesar.

Jesus answered, "You would have no power over me if my father did not give it to you from above. Therefore, the one who handed me over to you is guilty of a greater sin."

John 19:11

Or do you think that I cannot appeal to My Father, and He will at once put at My disposal more than twelve legions of angels?

Matthew 26:53

So why are we in such a broken state all over? Man, as usual, wants the power and influence of man instead of using the power of God given through his power and might.

"If you are not Born Again with the Holy Spirit, then you are under the Law, inside of Jesus is the fulfillment of the law through mercy and grace. According to scripture, Jesus states I am the way, the truth, and the light, and he is the only way."

GOD HAS GIVEN YOU POWER BECAUSE HE IS ALIVE IN YOU

John 14
Jesus Comforts His Disciples

1 Let not your heart be troubled: ye believe in God, also believe in me.

2 In my Father's house are many mansions: if it were not so, I would have told you. I go to prepare a place for you.

3 And if I go and prepare a place for you, I will come again, and receive you unto myself; where I am, there ye may also be.

4 And whither I go ye know, and the way ye know.

Jesus the Way to the Father

5 Thomas said to him, "Lord, we don't know where you are going, so how can we know the way?" 6 Jesus answered, "I am the way and the truth and the life. No one comes to the Father except through me. 7 If you know me, you will know my father as well. From now on, you do know him and have seen him."

8 Philip said, "Lord, show us the Father, and that will be enough for us." 9 Jesus answered: "Don't you know me, Philip, even after I have been among you such a long time? Anyone who has seen me has seen the father. So how can you say, 'Show us the father'?

10 Don't you believe that I am in the father and that the father is in me? The words I say to you I do not speak on my authority. Instead, it is the father, living in me, who is doing his work. 11 Believe me when I say that I am in the father and the father is in me, or at least believe in the evidence of the works themselves.

12 Very truly, I tell you, whoever believes in me will achieve the same as I have been doing and will do even greater things than these because I am going to the father. 13 And I will do whatever you ask in my name so that in the Son the Father is glorified. 14 You may ask me for anything in my name, and I will do it.

Jesus Promises the Holy Spirit

15 "If you love me, keep my commandments. 16 And I will ask the Father, and he will give you another advocate to help you and be with you forever— 17 the Spirit of truth. The world cannot accept him because it neither sees him nor knows him. But you know him, for he lives with you and will be in you.

18 I will not leave you as orphans; I will come to you. 19 Before long, the world will not see me anymore, but you will see me. Because I live, you also will live. 20 On that day, you will realize that I am in my father, and you are in me, and I am in you. 21 Whoever has my commands and keeps them is the one who loves me. My father will love the one who loves me, and I too will love them and show myself to them."

22 Then Judas (not Judas Iscariot) said, "But, Lord, why do you intend to show yourself to us and not to the world?"

23 Jesus replied, anyone who loves me will obey my teaching. My father will love them, and we will come to them and make our home with them. 24 Anyone who does not love me will not obey my teaching. These words you hear are not my own; they belong to the father who sent me.

25 "All this I have spoken while still with you. 26 But the Advocate, the Holy Spirit, whom the Father will send in my name, will teach you all things and will remind you of everything I have said to you.

27 Peace I leave with you; my peace I give you. I do not give to you as the world gives. Therefore, do not let your hearts be troubled, and do not be afraid.

28 "You heard me say, 'I am going away, and I am coming back to you.' If you loved me, you would be glad that I am going to the father, for the father is more significant than I. 29 I have told you now before it happens, so that when it does happen, you will believe.

30 I will not say much more to you, for the prince of this world is coming. He has no hold over me, 31, but he comes so that the world may learn that I love the father and do what my father has commanded me precisely.

Come now; let us leave.

CHAPTER 6

INSIDE GOD IS TOTAL FREEDOM FROM RELIGION TO FAITH

Let's examine this one at a time.

1. God Is.

   a. Who Is God? I Am.

2. Jesus Came Back to receive us.

   b. Jesus, crucified, dead, buried, and arose, with hundreds of witnesses.

3. God sent a New Covenant with The Birth of Jesus Christ.

   c. *"And I will give them one heart, and I will put a new spirit within you, and I will remove the stony heart out of their flesh and will give them a heart of flesh; that they may walk in My statutes, and keep My ordinances, and do them; and they shall be My people, and I will be their God."*

   (Ezk 36:26)

4. Gods Promises.

   d. Joshua 21:45 firmly establishes this truth: God keeps his word. There have never been any broken promises of God, not before Joshua, not after, and not now.

   e. For as many as are the promises of God, in Christ, they are [all answered] "Yes." So, through Him, we say our "Amen" to the glory of God. 2 Corinthians 1:2

I believe that I have confidence that Jesus and God with the Holy Spirit are one and that Jesus came. I believe him without a doubt. My book is not religious. I'm just telling you who I think is the creator and savior and why I know the truth, in my opinion, in my Spirit.

I don't care who you follow; all I know is that the God you serve better know Jesus, in my opinion. But if he doesn't, well, that's your prerogative. So I'm not trying to get you to believe in me; I'm trying to get you to believe in yourself so that you can walk in absolute power and control through a belief.

Believe what you want, and you have every right to follow your heart, mind, and soul; in the end, they all will end up in the same place. So again, I say, believe it. Don't waiver one bit. If you know for sure, that's what will be your foundation. So, live by it, stand on it and be immovable. Again, I am not the judge of you, but the words do it without my opinion.

No one can 100% stake their claim that their faith is the gold standard of all truth, except the Faith holder's own belief. There are 4200 religions, which probably is not all of them, but I chose that Jesus is the only way for me and my household. I can testify that the Lord Jesus Christ has healed me personally of many sicknesses and diseases. My wife was terminal. After nine years, the doctors still treat her and do not understand why she is alive with a rare terminal illness when they gave her one to ten days to live. When you accept Jesus, the comforter comes as a package deal. When you understand the relationship as co-tenants, everything changes. It's real power.

I am not your judge, and I cannot say that you are right or wrong. These are not religious matters but personal matters. Your beliefs are yours to accept and yours alone to follow. The facts are clear; we are controlled by whatever we accept as our truth. How we manage the information we receive is used for our thinking.

We make affirmations based on manifestation; teaching us these declarations will cause this material to appear in our hands. All manifestations begin with the images you have released into your subconscious mind on reality-based truths.

Faith does not consider your capabilities; it is the clarity of your understanding of faith. The interpretation of intelligence knows how to use information. The key to solving any problem is developing your strengths to manage your weaknesses, always expecting predictable results.

We have been God-given authority from the Garden and authorized to use it. God gave Adam the power and never relinquished it. God is the supreme higher Intelligence and does not change; that would imply fallibility if he did. Believing in the power within yourself is vital if you want those promises to be fulfilled. Most have doubts when things don't happen just as they had planned. Jesus said on the cross as he left his body; it's finished.

He ultimately left everything to you after the crucifixion, even though he hadn't risen. But he knew that he completed what we needed to reconstruct the connection to his spiritual and physical relationships. You are living in the promise and his covenant. His power set you free from the bondage of a broken spiritual connection with him. He restored the management of Adam's authority through the cross, in my opinion, because Adam was the manager and God the creator.

It is about time that we pick up where Adam left off. But we have a better plan, a new covenant, and promises under a mercy and grace plan. We can call it today a 401K, Social Security, etc.

Suppose we were to go through the Old Testament and read all the stories and episodes; Imagine the confusion and the questionable situations that might arise. However, one thing that did happen was Jesus came here as the Son of man, and Just over two thousand years ago, Jesus was crucified, died, was buried, and rose from the grave. There are records and witnesses of the birth, death, and resurrection. But, according to our Bible Scholars, Teachers, Ministers, and others, it is just over six thousand years ago in the timeline of Adam to today. But according to Carbon Dating, we had a real problem with time.

When we look through science and technology, it makes us wonder about what to believe. Jesus answered, "I am the way, the truth, and the life." I committed to following the scriptures, and I don't need God or Jesus to prove anything else. He is God and God alone; there is where I rest my faith.

"Jesus saith unto him, I am the way, the truth, and the life: no man cometh unto the Father, but by me."(John 14:6 KJV), So rather than going through a fight over something that cannot represent a total truth as a direct witness, men put these men on a pedestal to represent a power they do not have from God, neither do most understand.

We look to logic and man's mind to interpret these conflicting stories throughout the Bible and give us answers as though they were there. And we depend on men to clarify when they do not know or understand, nor have the authority. Many will even correct you as if they have the gold standard of God's word and an exclusive. So when I read "trust in God" and "every man is a lie," I see the warning of flashing red lights from God.

There are many religions but one God over them all so, they can't all be right, and they can't all be wrong, but to the believer of his faith, they are right. Final analysis, somebody is lying. The scripture states, "Not at all! Let God be true, and every human being is a liar." It's written, "So that you may be proven right when you speak and prevail when you judge." Romans 3:4

Our faith is not something that should be on a moving scale. When a project has a start, it also has a finish. It has a beginning and an ending. It is complete, done, and over. So, there is no new beginning; it is just a "pick-up and goes with it." Our job is to manage what God has created through our faith. So, the most significant benefit is understanding the value of your time here, and that it is minimal, I might add.

WEALTH AND POWER OF TIME

When you understand the value of giving time an assignment, it is power over all creation; It is not a measurement; it is an asset from God to man. More priceless than diamonds, platinum, gold, and silver. The benefits are immeasurable; It is the most valuable asset you have when you use it correctly. When you use a "Time Assignment," it places a hold on the power of the EGO and regulates pride more than anything. It stops anxiety and implements a standard of self-control. Time is irreplaceable, not like other securities, stocks, bonds, and commodities.

The ability to manage one's time effectively or productively is called time management. A "Time Assignment" is a tool of purpose; you open the doors of unlimited possibilities. However, time management is not like "Time Assignments." Time Assignments use time as an asset rather than a measurement of time. Assignments are unlimited opportunities whereby management is a measurement of space. A person who measures time looks to his wallet to see his increase; someone who uses Time Assignments looks to his watch for more opportunities.

Your mission is not to bleed into other works with time; they are independent of the different parts and not associated. To do so is the same as co-mingling funds of different clients for various projects. No attention is given to that task until the task is due. With this awareness of the value of time, you limit your time to only what is in the scope of your work or what you deem is practical and vital. In retrospect, if you do not value your time, no one else will. People will waste it, steal or disrespect it.

Time is the most significant wealth you will ever possess. It is the Commodity that exceeds all securities and asset value, whereby unlimited wealth is possible. When you understand how much time you have used in 24 hours, you see time in a whole new way. And when you view it by the seconds, you will know how wealthy you are; it's almost like cutting a piece of your favorite pie. In 24 hours, there are 86,400 seconds. So, when assigning a task to time, the value goes through the roof.

Suppose you have no time to assign, then you are already bankrupt. The key is to allocate prime tasks in slots you want to work for you. Prioritize your project in the importance of value to time, not to dollars. Don't cross lines in time with unrelated projects. Know what the allocation represents. If you are working, work. If you are resting, rest. If you are in the office, focus on why you are there. It's not time you steal from your employer with frivolous breaks. If you are on vacation, leave the business behind.

The world does not stop revolving because of your absences. Let's be clear here; most people look in their wallets and purse to see how much money they have or credit available on a credit card. Well, I look at my watch to see how much time I have. What I have in my wallet cannot compare to the unlimited possibilities the value of my time can yield. My wealth is in my time.

You must give an assignment to your time because the subconscious mind is busy responding to the images that your conscious mind constantly sends, and it is ready for action. However, the subconscious mind is not idly sitting; it is continuously building on the ideas and desires of the host.

Taking your thoughts into captivity.

Please do not take your mind lightly; it is more complex than the most complex supercomputers put together. When we allocate time as a task, it creates a pit stop to slow the mind down to perform maintenance, remove viruses and mental debris, and guards against misuse.

We must take every thought into captivity. If that does not happen, the Ego eagerly awaits as a poser and represents a topical response with echoes of its authority. It's puffed up and full of pride; it is the father of all arguments, built on the framework of an autoresponder.

When assigning tasks to time, we place a placeholder on events, circumstances, control anxiety, and unsolicited requests for our time. The Ego wants to be the administrator and present itself as robust. Therefore, assignments implement a standard for self-control to keep the Ego in check.

"Casting down imaginations, and every high thing that exalteth itself against the knowledge of God, and bringing into captivity every thought to the obedience of Christ." **(2 Corinthians 10:5 KJV)**

From the natural perspective of man's quest to interpret and understand the philosophies and ideologies of life, we create systematic concepts and flows to give us perspective and a point of view capable of explaining the who, what, when, and where of ideas.

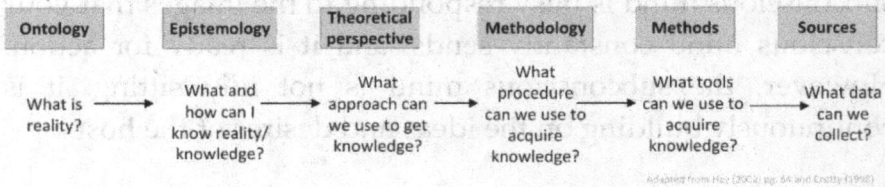

Ontology	Epistemology	Theoretical perspective	Methodology	Methods	Sources
What is reality?	What and how can I know reality/ knowledge?	What approach can we use to get knowledge?	What procedure can we use to acquire knowledge?	What tools can we use to acquire knowledge?	What data can we collect?

Adapted from Hay (2002) pg. 64 and Enctly (1998)

The whole reality is the footing to support the foundation of a core belief system. Footing is the source of all support, not the foundation as one might believe. It is hard for most of us to fathom a footing since most are unseen. However, the footing on a solid surface is stable, so the foundation will not shift under a load. When we see the foundation, it is appealing and carefully crafted to accommodate the facade of the building that will sit on it. The truth we are seeking is a belief acceptable to the fact from where all realities stem. The answer to that is what you will believe.

Belief systems come from all types of information inflows of correlating circumstances, the first being religion, culture, family, social networks, environment, and economic resources. Until we have established a footing for our belief to anchor, we cannot commit to any direction. That is the hollowness of man's heart that creates uncertainty, which is the basis for loyalty. Therefore, understanding what you believe is paramount to everything else on the planet.

You will see the tools you have to manage your universe and the authority to rule your space with divine support by a higher intelligence unmatched by anyone or anything. That power is in you. When you get to accepting who you are, all possibilities are available and ready for your use. However, thousands of years have gone by for this generation, inundated with misinformation and seeking out the mysterious. Yes, you are peculiar but also empowered by God.

SPEAKERS, COACHES, AND TEACHERS
BLIND LEADING THE BLIND

There are many great motivational speakers, and many have opened their minds to unlimited successes of human development. But, unfortunately, even though there are great successes, many users who seek out motivational speakers, coaches, and self-development teachers usually end up the same as big prize lottery winners.

No matter how much they win, they cannot sustain their newfound wealth. The primary reason is the lack of the principles of finance and wealth. Equally important is maintaining self-empowerment after the initial rush of excitement is gone. They do not understand the footing to support the new foundation.

Understanding how to integrate all the pieces to have a stable mindset and constant focus is very challenging when the core of your knowledge is from a shallow base. What plagues the guru's teaching self-development is most of them are feeding off each other's information. To them, it is just a business.

They lack the actual intellectual properties of the core of the belief. There is nothing new under the sun, even what I speak, except the concept and how to use it; they do not realize the link between mental, physical, and spiritual development.

To accept the journey of enlightenment into self-awareness and free from false teaching and cult-like following, you must first face the reality of the current state of what is real and what is not faith. Fear of being without God is the beginning of knowledge. Don't mistake thinking I am an island, but be aware that you can have the island all to yourself and be happy. But without God, there is no hope, period.

Let me first qualify that the brain is not the mind. The mind is not the brain, and the brain is a host and storage facility. The brain requires instructions and input that come from the conscious to the subconscious. The totality of the intellect consists of three parts, Conscious, Sub Conscious, and Ego. They are complex enough, but to be born without a user's manual further complicates human comprehension of self.

We must understand how to open the combination of mental, (faculties) physical, (senses), and spiritual fusion (faith) to integrate the five identified laws such as universal, natural, spiritual, success, and personal. Divine revelation knowledge opens secret doors to the mind and access to knowledge of a ready mind, and all possibilities are released.

Generations have come and gone, and the human species struggles through life. We have no idea of purpose and answers to events that take place in our lives. What actions do we take? What is the answer? These are things that we seemingly have no control over. We do something and do them again and don't know why.

We continue to repeat this loop, knowing that it is not our intent. We have no answers until now. But our children will suffer the same fate because we do not understand. We must seek out the truth for the benefit of our children, to leave them a productive and constructive life. Now you can share knowledge for a happy and abundant life.

We must teach our children life lessons and why it's essential to understand what it means to be human and born with a purpose. The answers in life are already present in the code of life. But where is this code, how do we get, and how do we use it? It is available to every human regardless of who you are, what race you are, and your religion. There are simply no hindrances that bar you from achieving your goal in life.

Self-awareness and belief will open the door to understanding. We have the keys to abundant life and the answers to the questions we've asked. Parents cannot pass down to their children what they do not know or understand. The principles created by our higher intelligence give us equal access to unlimited possibilities, absolute power, and control that only you and you alone can utilize.

I've heard expressions by others speaking of motivational speakers using language such as locksmiths of the mind. Still, most are repackaging old ideas and mostly saying what everyone else is saying, feeding themselves quotes from the past. Master Managers Handbook is the codebreaker to your infinite intelligence and self-replicating knowledge. True enlightenment that unlocks real power and success.

There have been many contributions in history that are instrumental in helping me along the way. Too many greats to mention; they all had spiritual inclinations and social and economic insights that have been invaluable. The laws are immovable and sovereign. Without the knowledge and use of these laws, you cannot accomplish anything. These laws bring what we most desire, such as peace, happiness, and joy.

They all work together and in harmony when understood. Suppose your desire is a path to immediate accelerated change that is permanent? Then you now hold the keys of every hope you desire in your hands.

Let's examine what most of us use to create instant and somewhat positive change, even though not lasting. It has many names including paradigm shift, manifestation, personal development, etc.

Paradigms: A paradigm shift is a significant change when a new and different way Changes how we think or act usually.

Paradigms only work when there is enough pain; when the pain is gone, so is the transition. Look at it this way. Let's assume you have a glass top stove, the type that's instant on and instant off. When you turn it off does not mean that the burner is cold. It just means that the power to keep it hot is gone. So, you walk over without realizing that the stove was just on. Even though your partner turns it off, and you put your hand on the burner, thinking it's off.

Instantly the moment you touch your reaction is instantaneous as you remove your hand from the burner. Without any thought, it was an instant response to maximum pain. That's a paradigm. As soon as the pain is gone, you continue as though nothing happened. But you are now more aware of the stove's possibilities of injury. So, you keep that knowledge, and it becomes surface knowledge imprinted by pain. So now, the movement is called a paradigm shift.

Why the Master Managers Handbook is superior is it creates perception and anticipation. You change inside your head through philosophy and ideology. Your mind learns to use fundamental mental tools. Your newfound way of thinking you instantly get. Paradigms work but don't last. It's like water — it quenches the thirst. When you walk in the real power of the comforter that's inside of you, if you have accepted Jesus Christ, you would understand the meaning of not ever being hungry and never thirsting means.

Thousands of people are pushing paradigm-shifting programs all because it helps you to recognize what is obvious. It makes you look at your pain; it makes you think about your pain and focus on it, but how do you fix a lasting pain? It's a big-time commercialized money-making gig. It works, but it is temporary. Some continue thriving from the paradigm shift as is, but there is always a need for recharging.

Let's look at the Lion.

God makes the Lion with Adam's mindset; Adam comes into this world created in the image of God, with no fear, no doubt, no worries, and autonomous authority to rule. The Lion is the first to recognize actual power and lead over time. He uses it very well. All his actions are intentional, direct, and calculated. He knows the order and his directive to survive and provides for his pack. The Lion does not waste time on anything unrelated to the security of the lioness and cubs.

He recognizes his authority in the jungle, even though self-appointed, he is willing to die for the purpose to rule, not as Adam failed in the Garden and was evicted in today's terms, by God (I AM), not the Sheriff's office. He's not interested in anything else except these three things, eats, mate, and rest. When he eats, he eats; when it's time to rest, the Lion sleeps up to 21 hours; when it's time to mate, he mates. In his mind, the jungle is his property and his playground. If you enter the jungle, you are in his domain.

The Lion knows that he must always be agile and always ready when the opportunity comes up, so he takes precautions by managing his strength, speed, tactics by improving his skills. The intended purpose is his only interest. He only uses what is necessary to complete each task, and He is an expert in time assignments. Every action taken is measured and controlled by him. He is the master of anticipation. Though he sleeps long hours, nothing gets by his vibrations because he intones with the universe. (Nature)

The Lion knows he is not the biggest, the fastest, the smartest, nor the strongest. But he has two things to his advantage, fearless and purpose. The Lion feels autonomous just as Adam was given this authority at creation. The Lion is a poser, and he can only imitate man's rule; God only gave that to Adam and his descendants. As mighty as the Lion may be, compared to man, with all his uniqueness, his ambitions are more significant even though his heart is half the size of man's.

Because of Lion's philosophy, when he walks into any part of the jungle, the animals stop and notice his presence, and when they see him as a predator, he sees them as prey. Everything creeping, crawling, and all creatures on land, air, and water are all game. To him, it's his buffet. He can eat anything in the environment he chooses. He feels entitled because of his perceived authority.

He does everything Adam has the authority to do, which is to subdue. But the Lion has given them all the same name, "Food." The Lion bows down to nothing in the jungle, and he is always willing to put up a good fight, even if it means dying. He does not let Adam's designation get in the way of his purpose, which is to eat.

But in his spirit and heart, he knows that the man is the true ruler, and he is like a thief, a fox guarding the henhouse without permission. For this reason, is why man can tan this fearless beast of power. Man has absolute authority from God to subdue, and the Lion is not exempt from being ruled. (Gen 1:28)

Because God has not given us the spirit of fear but of power, might, and a sound mind. (2 Tim 1:7)

BLIND LEADING THE BLIND

'"THESE PEOPLE HONOR ME WITH THEIR LIPS, BUT THEIR HEART IS FAR AWAY FROM ME. AND IN VAIN DO THEY WORSHIP ME, TEACHING AS DOCTRINES THE COMMANDMENTS OF MEN."'

After Jesus called the crowd to Him, He said to them, "Hear and understand! 11It is not what enters the mouth that defiles the person, but what comes out of the mouth; this defiles the person."

Then the disciples came and said to Him, "Do You know that the Pharisees were offended when they heard this statement?" But He answered and said, "Every plant which My heavenly Father did not plant will be taken up by its roots. So, leave them alone; they are blind guides of blind people. And if a person who is blind guides another who is blind, both will fall into a pit."

YOURS FOR THE ASKING

I ask God why so many people have so much money and waste it. The answer came rather quickly. They wanted it; they believe they could have it. And they got it. We are the creators of our script. You are the artist; brush to canvas, every detail comes from our vision, as so many have said before. The truth is our minds work in pictures. Be fruitful and multiply. The prayer of Jabez, 1 Chronicles 4:10, is the perfect example of expectations of the promise by faith.

THE WILL OF GOD

All that the Father giveth me shall come to me, and he that cometh to me I will cast out in no wise. For I came down from heaven, not to do my own will, but the will of him that sent me. And this is the father's will which hath sent me, that of all which he hath given me, not one will be lost, but should raise again at the last day. And this is the will of him that sent me, that every one which seeth the Son, and believeth on him, may have everlasting life: and I will raise him at the last day. John 6:36-40

Who desires all men to be saved and to come unto the knowledge of the truth. 1 Timothy 2:4

The Jews then murmured at him because he said, I am the bread which came down from heaven. And they said, Is not this Jesus, the Son of Joseph, whose parents we know? How is it then that he saith, I came down from heaven? Jesus therefore answered and said unto them, Murmur not among yourselves. John 6:41-43

CHAPTER 7

FREUD'S MODEL OF THE HUMAN MIND

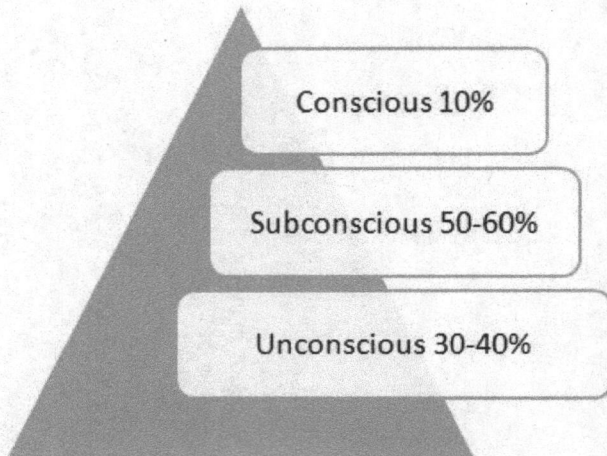

Conscious 10%

Subconscious 50-60%

Unconscious 30-40%

Philosophically speaking, the mind may well refer to one's personality, identity, and memories. The mind is a site of spiritual awareness for the religious and is the generator of ideas for the scientist. It carries with it a variety of labels. Mind references were in the beginning metaphorical. In the 14th and 15th centuries, the generalization of the mind to include all mental faculties thought, volition, emotion, and memory gradually developed.

The late 19th and early 20th centuries saw psychology become a respected science. Following Freud's work and the work of others, the mind/body question and the role of the mind became popular topics. Almost always today, the concept of the mind and its function is discussed from a scientific perspective.

Freud's Conscious Mind

When we define consciousness as awareness of something, describing the human mind only as recalled must seem simple enough to qualify only those activities we can remember as our own.

This view faces two challenges. In the first place, only about 10% of the mind's work consists of conscious thought, and in the second place, this approach does not explain how random events come into existence.

http://journalpsyche.org/understanding-the-human-mind/

There are two functions that the conscious mind is capable of addressing:

A) Its ability to direct your focus.

B) Its ability to imagine that which is not real

The conscious mind is an essential part of the triad of the human mind, as it serves as a scanner. A human mind will perceive an event, trigger a reaction; you store the event in your subconscious or unconscious. Dependent upon the magnitude of the event, it will remain there for as long as is necessary.

Freud's Subconscious Mind:

The subconscious stores recent memories that you need to recall quickly, such as your telephone number or the name of a new acquaintance. Additionally, it contains current information you use every day, such as your current thoughts, behavior patterns, habits, and feelings.

It is the mind's random-access memory (RAM) that works in Freud's subconscious mind. As a result, the unconscious mind can be viewed as the source of dreams and automatic thoughts (those that spontaneously arise without apparent reason), as the repository of forgotten memories (which may still be accessible to consciousness in the future), and as a repository of implicit knowledge. ("the things we do without thinking") that we have mastered."

Freud's Unconscious Mind: (EGO)

Memory and past experiences are stored in the unconscious mind. Traumatic memories and those that have been consciously forgotten and are no longer essential to us (automatic thoughts) have been repressed. Nevertheless, we still form beliefs, habits, and behaviors from these memories and experiences.

Likewise, it is here that the Ego is located since it responds by defending itself or puffing itself up with pride. Just like a computer program, it is quick to remember past hurts that repressed traumatic circumstances.

An analysis of the previous illustration shows that the unconscious sits below the subconscious in the mind. Despite the intimate connection between the subconscious and unconscious, the unconscious mind is where all one's memories, habits, and behaviors are held, like an underground library, if you will. This is the repository of all your deep-seated emotions that have been programmed in you since birth. Thus, I think that Freud's interpretations of human behavior are generally correct, but in my view, the heart serves as the library of the mind.

According to Freud's psychoanalytic theory, it is in the unconscious mind that change can take place.

The Bible dealt with this long before Freud's existence and the Egyptians with the Eye of Horus. Yet, from a religious perspective, we are told to have the mind of Christ. And many theologians fail to understand the interpretation fully and lack the knowledge to understand the presence of the Holy Spirit in man.

1 Corinthians 2:9-16

9. But as it is written, Eye hath not seen, nor ear heard, neither have entered the heart of man, the things which God hath prepared for them that love him.

10. But God hath revealed them unto us by his Spirit: for the Spirit searcheth all things, yea, the deep things of God. 11. For what man knoweth the things of a man, save the spirit of man which is in him? Even so, the things of God knoweth no man, but the Spirit of God. 12. So now we have received, not the spirit of the world, but the spirit which is of God; that we might know the things that are freely given to us of God. 13. So we also speak, not in the words which man's wisdom teacheth, but the Holy Ghost teacheth; comparing spiritual things with spiritual.

14. But the natural man receiveth, not the things of the Spirit of God: for they are foolishness unto him: neither can he know them, because they are spiritually discerned. 15. But he that is spiritual judgeth all things, yet he himself is judged of no man. 16. For who hath known the mind of the Lord, that he may instruct him? But we have the mind of Christ.

God made it possible for all his believers to enjoy the power of his presence on earth to endure during our time here.

THE MIND AND THE BRAIN

Human Brain Anatomy

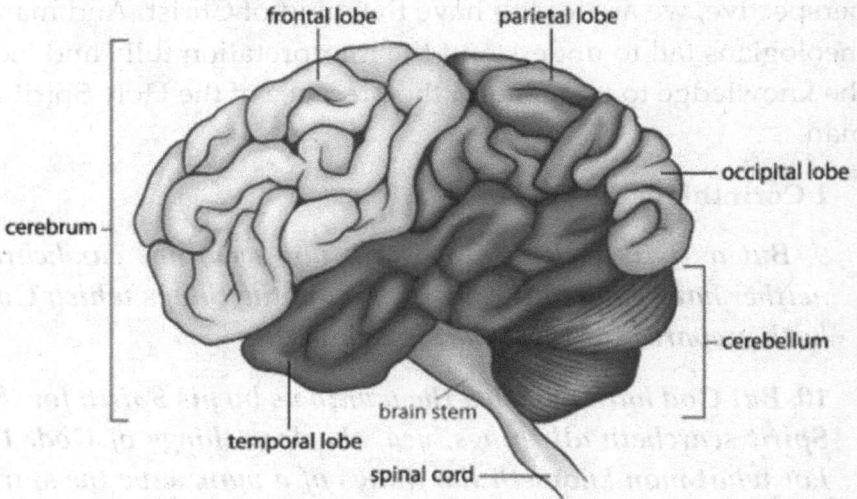

frontal lobe

parietal lobe

occipital lobe

cerebrum

cerebellum

brain stem

temporal lobe

spinal cord

MIND TRAFFIC FLOWCHART:

It is insanity to drive a super-fast car at the highest speed without a steering wheel. First, if you have never been trained to operate, it would be a futile mistake. Yet many do just that. But the birthing of a human being is precisely what happens as we enter this world. We are born without a manual, and as we journey through life, we only receive fragments of information, enough to barely survive or sufficient to make informed decisions. Even at the highest levels of education, there is a void that is never filled.

It is not enough to believe you are knowledgeable, but it would be better to understand what you think and believe in what you know. Right or wrong, belief becomes your foundational truth, and it is always the center of all interactions to keep you balanced. Many of us find Religion or follow a cultural tradition as an appearance of faith, but they are not rooted and established. Hence, they have nothing to anchor to. Nothing can fill this emptiness until you understand what true spiritual enlightenment and a real power you are learned to create desires into physical assets.

Our consciousness is always seeking out opportunities, and unknowingly, the mental framework is preloaded programs, and system functions are automatic and self-engaging. So, it is to your advantage to learn the steps of the cognitive processes. The mental stimuli create vibrations as the conscious awakens to the subconscious and Ego. However, we have not been taught how to incorporate our tools; neither have we identified them nor utilized them. I have charted and determined the flow and the laws we must harness to exercise their power; these laws are our programs.

It gets down to the single most crucial question, what do you believe, because everything about you begins there in your core belief system. Belief is everything, and it is the engine of the soul. Your internal is not regulated by what someone else thinks; you are the host; it all rides on you. That is why you need to develop, understand and know its use. When your belief requires you to act, it is your reaction.

Best you have control over the response. If you knew the world we live in, although created by God but controlled by men, you might view things very differently, and you should. What matters more than anything in life is that you live by your convictions and not someone else's expectations. Understanding why you believe and what you believe is the vehicle for your purpose.

Let's look at the beginning of our traffic flow as it completes the interpersonal mind traffic loop. But, first, we have to understand the functionality of the breakdown of the flow of information processing to determine corrective action; instead, the sensory system picks up external conditions, then merges with the six faculties of the mind.

The "Will" generally is the deciding factor but not always the first prong of the faculties to interact with the pulse. The "Will" triggers the core beliefs system. It operates through the five laws, which are programs; they are the mainframe because they are skeletal of all immovable actions but must be used in conjunction with our faculties — learning to adapt to these increases exponential success and accelerates immediate change.

Utilizing the six faculties will enable you to create a flow and control by adopting core beliefs. Conflict resolution gives you the ability to manage anxiety, worry, unsolicited opinions, and drama management. "Time Assignments" are the most critical step and essential part of the resolution process. The very first action you must take is to accept or reject the pulse and determine if it is friend or foe. Bear in mind the subconscious mind does not contradict any signal or impulse by origin. Its actions are controlled only by receiving and responding to create the picture or image until resolve happens. All of this occurs instantaneously before the conscious mind accepts this information into the subconscious mind.

It operates as your onboard autoresponder, and its network of backlinks is constantly building the picture. If this step is miss, the Ego is waiting to show its ugly head. Its programs generally operate from the unconscious mind. The past hurts and trauma waiting to be triggered always essential for its boastful pride and lead to self-preservation; these vibrations are stimuli to your core that send the signals back to the conscious for output. Bear in mind your ability to understand and identify your tools is key to the entire process, just as a carpenter uses tools to create and complete a project; however complex, tools for the job have to be identified to determine use and outcome. In reality, your toolbox consists of:

1. The sensory system hardware

2. The faculties software

3. The five laws mainframe and programs

4. Conflict resolution system

5. Time assignments

6. Core belief systems

7. Forgiveness(memory lane triggers)

Remember, what you have allowed passing through will yield the byproduct of the thought. Good or bad, it was our choice.

Let us first recognize what we have by nature:

MIND=CARNAL+FACULTIES+EGO

BODY=PHYSICAL

SPIRIT=SOUL

Then we have.

CONSCIOUS=RECEIVER (The interface of your sensory system.)

SUBCONSCIOUS=STORAGE

EGO=AUTORESPONDER=ADMINISTRATOR **(Some say unconscious, I disagree)**

The conscious is a monitoring station, and it's the processor of the sensory signals system. The system is designed with **five antennas as follows:**

SIGHT; Power of Seeing

TOUCH; Act of Touching something

TASTE; A Sensation of Flavors

HEARING; Perceiving Sound

SMELL; Perceiving Odors or Scents

These make up our physical body's hardware as sensors that read all external physical and environmental conditions.

After the sensors pick up any signals, it instantly sends this information to the faculties; they read the data as a scan and merge for a deposit into the subconscious mind. Before data is sent to the subconscious, it must accept or reject the data. Bear in mind the subconscious cannot determine if it is real or unreal, good or bad. So, it is your opportunity to shield your subconscious from receiving and processing an undesirable outcome. If you want your return to be positive, accept positive; if you want it to be negative, accept negative. Whatever you allow to pass into your subconscious will be returned to the sender.

There is a significant opportunity to accept or reject. Based on your by-laws with the mental anchors that created the triggers, the core belief system will trigger a response to accept or reject. This is where conflict resolution can empower the process thought unitizing a tool called forgiveness. You can reset with forgiveness, and it's a tool you will reset and continue or reject just the same. But it, in a sense, empties your trash bin. Mental debris happens when we allow drama and unforgiveness to linger on and become baggage. This empowers you to keep your systems clean and balanced.

Best to push the reset and decide early. It keeps your mind clear and keeps situations from spiraling out of control. In addition, doing so gives you control over the entire mental process. Finally, your options are accepted and support the association, reject and dis-associate, reject and discontinue, reject the idea and continue the relationship.

The subconscious mind and the Ego simultaneously send to the torso core signals and vibration at this point. The faculties have read the [conscious] [subconscious], then pass this information to the Ego; these are desires, pictures, passion, triggers, lust, pride, greed, selfishness, anger, bitterness, prejudices, etc. Thus, vibrations simultaneously return to the conscious in the form of an emotional impulse even though it all originated from the hardware that senses the external.

The conscious and the Ego respond to all mind traffic; together, they accept or reject. Be very mindful of the Ego; it is puffed up, self-centered, and full of pride. The Reset Button is forgiveness and acceptance and rejection as well. Let me be clear; the "Reset Button is the joystick of your interactions with "The Will." The most powerful tool you have is to accept, reject and forgive. All these actions keep your mind clear of reaping

95

the harvest of mental debris, viruses, and malware into our character's good nature and making decisions that are not options

In the faculties, you will find.

- **The Will; Carnal/Spirit**
- **Reasoning; Action of Thinking**
- **Intuition; Instinctual Feeling**
- **Memory; Mind Storage**
- **Imagination; New Ideas, Images, and Concepts**
- **Perception; Perceiving and Observation**

They monitor the conscious emotion and filter the core belief system input.

The faculties will operate based on the core belief system, and the five laws will govern the entire loop.

LAWS OVERVIEW

The self-governance of the core belief system:

Laws are the Programs:

Universal: Principals by which everyone and everything in the Universe is governed. You cannot change in any way; The Universe exists in perfect harmony. You begin to align yourself once you understand the Universal Laws; you will experience transformation in every area of your life.

Natural: Law that is based on an in-depth understanding of human nature. It is human nature that consists of intrinsic values which can be devalued. It can be applied in either direction. As per natural law theory, everyone has the right to live.

Spiritual: The most important of the laws is the law whereby one becomes known to self. It is unique and about your well-being; it is the gate to all possibilities of perception. With this law, you have the keys to success and happiness; you will have a clearer picture of your place in the world — the birthplace of purpose.

Success: The second most important law is the law whereby you obtain unlimited possibilities through the formulas for success and the intellectual mindset of some of the greatest minds. The Bible states a wise man seeks many counselors. You may find these today in books and on the internet; YouTube is probably the greatest, along with Google. There you can find coaches and form virtual mastermind groups without ever leaving your home. You can see and learn about what makes the great-great. This information is free; many of them have transcended but left YOU a blueprint to follow. Success is your choice, and you have all the tools available to be successful.

Personal: These are the laws of personal commitment created by your by-laws of a core belief system; they are by no means associated with a class of people as some countries establish rights and religion. The anchors of your core belief system keep you centered from the sway of frivolous persuasion. Also, they are the pillars of self-control and development. This is where you set goals and affirm hope and follow your core belief system by-laws and affirmations.

Rules:

Reject what you do not want. Only accept what you do.

Never accept lack and poverty comments; reject from the onslaught.

"To control the traffic of the mind, you must take time with it; It is a twenty-lane highway congested and looking for exits. It is your supercomputer full of complexities waiting to be trained and disciplined." But you must slow it down and contain it with every word in subjection to guard its use.

Conflict resolution:

This is the master control, the subordinate to the "Will," and must be kept at bay from the Ego. By all intended purposes, it is the brakes to all actions, and the mental breakers or disconnection before any determination can cause harm to either party. It is the reset of thought and the lever to forgiveness.

Time Assignments:

When "Conflict Resolution" is involved, it requires that you make a decision. There are only two options, disassociates, or continues; the same pulse triggers vibrations as it returns to the conscious. Depending on the option chosen, a "Time Assignment" would be given to the issue. Do not allow the recycled unresolved situation to be in your subconscious mind.

Vibrations returning to the conscious have one response: act on the initial impulse of the first contact. Remember the determination you made to accept or reject. Reality and illusion are equal to the subconscious mind, whether they are good or bad. To allow it to flow into your core was an option you chose and was under your control.

98

It simply returns what you send out, and this is the product of return. It would help if you gave it an assignment. Give it a specific time and slot for resolution. Time is a tool and a release value for all pressure as a cool-down period that removes anxiety and maintains order in your mind. Just as a free radical causes damage to the body, uncontrolled drama causes damage to the mind.

We supercharge creative effectiveness when time is a measurement of space. Therefore, value time for the wealth it brings. You are the delegator of time and circumstances; the outcome will be more favorable if you decide.

Memory Lane:

Memory lane is not always an enjoyable trip; it is a place you should always proceed with caution. When we receive memory, it comes to us in the form of pictures. Simply because our mind works in pictures, and images are also attached to thoughts and thoughts to words. It is our responsibility to capture all these as if they were words spoken.

Past events become a mental library in our minds, like a CD containing music or a movie stored on a hard drive welded into the fabric of our mind. Our conscious captures the moment in a flash, jolts our subconscious, and triggers the unconscious mind; this is where the Ego resides.

These mind triggers happen by going to places that remind us of a moment in time. These moments can translate into happy, sad, or a not so good experiences. Unaware of the subliminal mental debris you may have opened, it can cause you to act out at a person you may be in a relationship with and once had forgiven. Best to stay away from this lane.

They don't understand what makes you upset or act out. The past shouldn't be relived as though it was yesterday or has just happened. The Ego thrives in the dead space because it has no passion except for its existence and works as an offline vault of past hurts, broken relationships, and suppressed trauma until the Ego makes its beckoning call. Then, pride awakens it with faults and venom.

Forgiveness:

Matthew 6:14-15 KJV, States; (14) For if ye forgive men their trespasses, your heavenly Father will also forgive you. (15) But if ye forgive not men their trespasses, neither will your heavenly Father forgive your trespasses.

Forgiveness is important because it releases the offensive situation, disables the Ego from activation, and cleanses your heart of debris. Forgiveness is also a form of self-love that can love yourself enough to free yourself from its entanglements. To release someone from the shame and feeling of Guilt is the most powerful tool to have to avoid and resolve conflict.

The benefits are immeasurable; anxiety, stress, and hostility are the key driver of physical breakdowns in the body. Drama alone can send your blood pressure through the roof and attacking your immune system. But, on the other hand, it helps you heal broken relationships and build self-esteem. The real downside to unforgiveness is holding it in your heart, and it takes a grip on your spirit, causing it to grieve and you become depressed.

Anytime we let unforgiveness take root in our conscience, we impregnate our subconscious mind with the imagination of desires creating all types of outcomes. Alternative ideas that are unruly can set a dangerous precedence that supports a lack of self-control. To master any situation, you must have self-control. Clearing the path to your destiny means that you must remove any negative underlying issues that inhibit your actions and decisions. Unforgiveness becomes a stronghold and destroys belief systems.

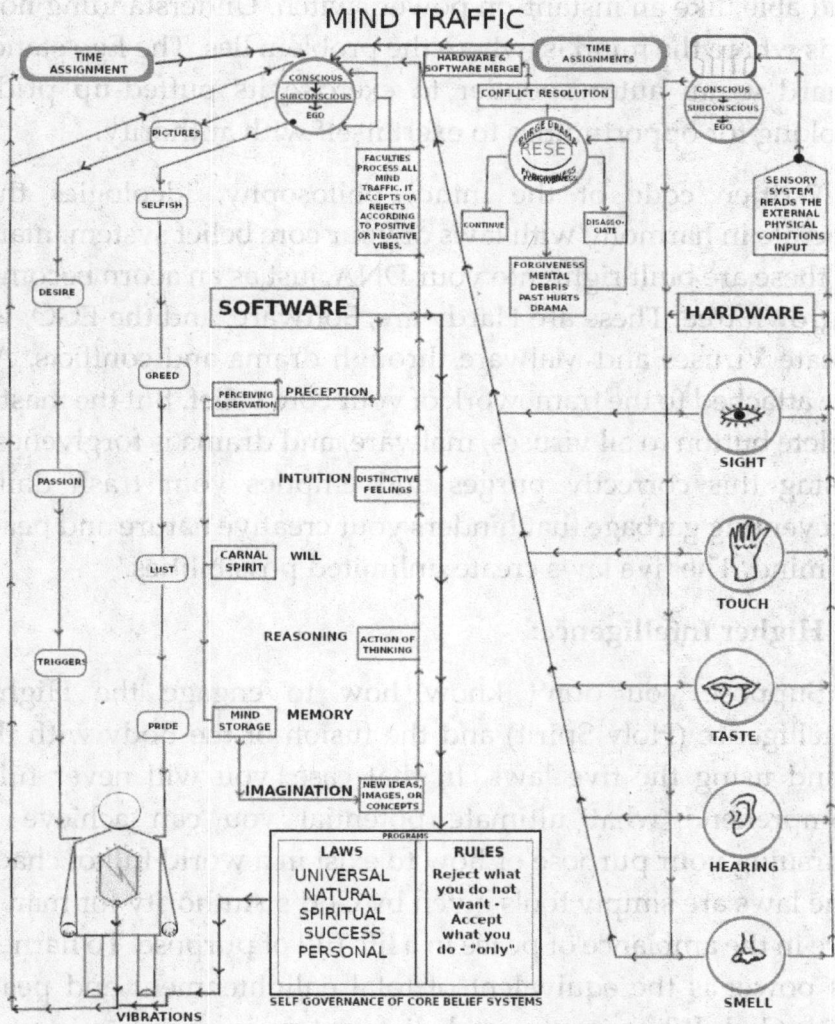

MIND TRAFFIC

TIME ASSIGNMENT

TIME ASSIGNMENTS

HARDWARE & SOFTWARE MERGE

CONSCIOUS SUBCONSCIOUS EGO

CONFLICT RESOLUTION

CONSCIOUS SUBCONSCIOUS EGO

PICTURES

FACULTIES PROCESS ALL MIND TRAFFIC. IT ACCEPTS OR REJECTS ACCORDING TO POSITIVE OR NEGATIVE VIBES.

PURGE DRAMA
RESE

SENSORY SYSTEM READS THE EXTERNAL PHYSICAL CONDITIONS INPUT

SELFISH

CONTINUE

DISASSO-CIATE

DESIRE

FORGIVENESS MENTAL DEBRIS PAST HURTS DRAMA

SOFTWARE

HARDWARE

GREED

PERCEIVING OBSERVATION

PRECEPTION

SIGHT

PASSION

INTUITION

DISTINCTIVE FEELINGS

LUST

CARNAL SPIRIT

WILL

TOUCH

REASONING

ACTION OF THINKING

TRIGGERS

TASTE

PRIDE

MIND STORAGE

MEMORY

IMAGINATION

NEW IDEAS, IMAGES, OR CONCEPTS

HEARING

PROGRAMS

LAWS
UNIVERSAL
NATURAL
SPIRITUAL
SUCCESS
PERSONAL

RULES
Reject what you do not want -
Accept what you do - "only"

SMELL

VIBRATIONS

SELF GOVERNANCE OF CORE BELIEF SYSTEMS

2021 COPYRIGHT PATRICK BARBER SR

MIND TRAFFIC FLOW CHART

THE FIVE LAWS OF COLLABORATION
UNIVERSAL, NATURAL, SPIRITUAL LAWS,
SUCCESS LAWS, PERSONAL LAWS

The mind is never idle and constantly communicates between the conscious, subconscious, and Ego. Ready, willing, and able, like an instant-on power switch. Understanding how to is where the mind is, where the problem lies. The Ego stands guard as an autoresponder to exercise its puffed-up pride, looking for opportunities to exert itself with authority.

Written code of the mind, philosophy, ideologies that operate in harmony with laws of your core belief system, many of these are built right into your DNA, just as an acorn becomes a grown tree. These are Hardware, Software, and the EGO; we create Viruses and Malware through drama and conflicts. All are attached to the framework of your core belief. But the master delete button to all viruses, malware, and drama is forgiveness. Using this correctly purges and empties your trash daily, preventing garbage that hinders your creative nature and peace of mind. The five laws create unlimited possibilities.

Higher Intelligence:

Suppose you don't know how to engage the Higher Intelligence (Holy Spirit) and the fusion of the Body with the mind using the five laws. In that case, you will never fully comprehend what ultimate potential you can achieve in pursuing your purpose or how to exist in a world full of chaos. The laws are simply tools given by God's Authority for man to live in the ambiance of peace in a life full of purpose. To harness its power is the equivalent of total enlightenment and peace with God. When your core belief system is complete in your understanding, the knowledge of existence is actual. Personal laws are self-imposed law requires accepting a core belief system. Your actions are anchoring to boundaries and by-laws of self-governance. Therefore, it would be best if you respected all the laws to work in harmony and balance.

FIVE LAWS OF LIFE: These are the Programs we must use.

1. **Universal laws (Not Optional)**

2. **Natural laws (Not Optional)**

3. **Spiritual laws (Free Will)**

4. **Success laws (Models and Pathways)**

5. **Personal laws. (Self-imposed)**

Harness these laws, release unlimited powers of self-awareness and create possibilities without boundaries. Understanding these forces are harmony and balance for enlightenment to purpose.

Know who you are, make an appointment with yourself, give time for an assignment. Take a little time with your mind. The less you understand about time, the more you are a slave to it.

You are Here

 — New Covenant

Before Crucifixion

Carnal

Void
Empty

After Crucifixion

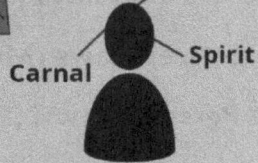

Free Will

Carnal

Spirit

5 Senses - Hardware

Sight
Hearing
Touch
Taste
Smell

5 Laws - Accessories

Universal   Success
Natural   Personal
Spiritual

6 Faculties - Software

* Will
* Reasoning
* Intuition
* Imagination
* Perception
* Memory

CHAPTER 8

UNIVERSAL LAWS

1. Law of divine oneness:

All other laws are built on the direction of divine oneness. In this law, we are all linked through creation.

Whereby confirms God is a collective of One. He means that everything we do has a ripple effect and impacts the collective—not just ourselves. To call upon this principle for self-improvement, remember that your actions both matter and make a difference. Wherever a person of faith with the Spirit of God is anywhere in the world, there is God.

There is one body and one spirit, just as you were called to one hope when the spirit of God called you; one Lord, one faith, one baptism; one God and Father of all, who is over all and through all and in all. (Ephesians 4:4-6 KJV) (I guess that's the 4200 plus religions, depending on their walk-in faith.)

2. Law of vibration:

There is a frequency and a vibration to everything in the universe. It is said that "nothing stands still, as everything is either being dragged toward someplace or pushed away from something." Furthermore, things that resonate with each other are attracted to one another. To manifest your desires using this law, you must match your vibration with what you want. (This can be called faith and focus)

3. Law of correspondence:

Habits are passed down via DNA-family ties and consciously taking steps to break them. (In my opinion, I call this the backlinks effect because the mind builds pictures, images and it continues that path until it completes the picture or gets some resolution).

4. Law of attraction:

"Many people fear that bad thoughts or low vibrations will somehow ruin their lives because they're unaware. Our self-worth and mindset are reflected in the law, not as a punishment. Despite past decisions you have made, you can make new decisions and attract different circumstances if you choose."

5. Law of inspired action:

You must take action to realize your dreams. Inspired action refers to taking action to make your dreams come true. (These are the steps whereby the Master Managers Handbook differs in the application; when you learn the tools of the mindset, you are in control of the attraction.)

6. Law of perpetual transmutation of energy:

You possess the capacity to move mountains within you just as a seed carries all its promise within its tiny shell.

Remember, small shifts equal significant results. (This action I agree with totally, but I would use only small positive things as goals to complete).

7. Law of cause and effect:

Whatever you put out—good or bad—you get right back. You will get an apple tree if you plant apple seeds. To harness the power of this law, you must be aware of how your actions and decisions affect not just yourself but also everyone around you and focus only on sending out positive vibes.

8. Law of compensation:

The law of compensation is about reaping what you sow. "It instills trust in us that we will be compensated for our work as long as we're open to receiving.

Don't be deceived: God is not mocked, for whatever one sows, he will also reap. **Galatians 6:7**

Compensation in this sense does not only mean financial rewards or employment arrangements. Instead, it's about receiving payment for everything you contribute to the world around you, including the love, joy, and kindness you spread.

9. Law of relativity:

"Everything has multiple expressions, and every situation or challenge has multiple perspectives." In other words, we assign meaning to things and can choose to view things as "bad" or as working out for us. (Just as you can use water for drinking or drowning).

10. Law of polarity:

Everything has an opposite: If there's an up, there's a down. If there's light, there's dark. One cannot exist without the other.

11. Law of perpetual motion:

Every single thing in this world is changing forever, and our role is to embrace that change. Appreciate the moment if things are going all right, but don't push it beyond the natural order of things.

12. The law of giving and receiving:

The energies of this law operate within all of us and create flow; they need to be in balance

NATURAL LAWS

When we understand the simplicity of things, we are free from the clutter of alternative thinking. But, unfortunately, too much thought can be confusing, a trap of sophistication and a measure of intelligence built to disguise true intentions.

Let's look at the benefits of non-resistance to natural laws.

The first example of natural laws is the universal acceptance that killing a human being is wrong. Two people can create a child and become the parents and natural caregivers of the child.

If we want to minimize their effects, other fundamental laws that no man can act upon but must adapt to the forces are Gravity, Centrifugal Force, Inertia, Kinetic Energy, and Friction. The excellent use of these is a very Productive life, Superior

Knowledge, Sociability, and Friendship. Thus, the two great commandments would sit above Spiritual and Natural laws.

SPIRITUAL LAWS

Master, which is the great commandment in the law? Jesus said unto him, Thou shalt love the Lord thy God with all thy heart, and with all thy soul, and with all thy mind. This is the first and great commandment. And the second is like, unto it, thou shalt love thy neighbor as thyself. On these two commandments hang all the law and the prophets."

Matthew 22:36-40, KJV

"By this shall all men know that ye are my disciples if ye have love one to another."

John 13:35, KJV

"As the Father hath loved me, so have I loved you: continue ye in my love. If ye keep my commandments, ye shall abide in my love; even as I have kept my father's commandments and abide in his love. These things have I spoken unto you, that my joy might remain in you, and that your joy might be complete. This is my commandment, That ye love one another, as I have loved you. Greater love hath no man than this that a man lay down his life for his friends."

John 15:9-13, KJV

"Owe no man anything, but to love one another: for he that loveth another hath fulfilled the law. For this, thou shalt not commit adultery, Thou shalt not kill, thou shalt not steal, Thou shalt not bear false witness, Thou shalt not covet; and if there be any other commandments, it is briefly comprehended in this saying; namely, thou shalt love thy

neighbor as thyself. Love worketh no ill to his neighbor: therefore, love is the fulfilling of the law."

Romans 13:8-10, KJV

"Now as touching things offered unto idols, we know that we all have knowledge. Knowledge puffeth up, but charity edifieth."

1 Corinthians 8:1, KJV

"But covet the best gifts earnestly: and yet shew I unto you a more excellent way."

1 Corinthians 12:31, KJV

"And though I have the gift of prophecy, and understand all mysteries, and all knowledge; and though I have all faith so that I could remove mountains, and have not charity, I am nothing . . . And now abideth faith, hope, charity, these three; but the greatest of these is charity."

1 Corinthians 13:2, 13, KJV

"For all the law is fulfilled in one word, even in this; Thou shalt love thy neighbor as thyself."

Galatians 5:14, KJV

"If ye fulfill the royal law according to the scripture, Thou shalt love thy neighbor as thyself; ye do well:"

James 2:8, KJV

"And above all things have fervent charity among yourselves: for charity shall cover the multitude of sins."

1 Peter 4:8, KJV

"He that loveth not knoweth not God; for God is love."

1 John 4:8, KJV

"And because iniquity shall abound, the love of many shall wax cold."

Matthew 24:12, KJV

SUCCESS LAWS

The 17 Laws of Success by Napoleon Hill

1 Definiteness of Purpose — Napoleon Hill said, "There is one quality which one must possess to win, and that is definiteness of purpose, the knowledge of what one wants, and a burning desire to possess it." Focus your actions and thoughts on one big and specific goal in life. You won't make progress you want to in life if you chase multiple, contradictory goals at a time.

2 Mastermind Alliance is the habit of working in complete harmony with others to attain a specific objective. So, when two minds come together, they'll get ideas that neither one of them would get by themselves. And the more knowledgeable people you work with, the better-quality ideas you'll get.

3 Going the Extra Mile — Napoleon Hill said, "Render more and better service than paid for, and sooner or later you will receive compound interest from your investment." If you're stuck at a certain level in life and want to make a lasting change, you'll need to take massive action in the direction you're trying to go and maintain a strong momentum.

4 Applied Faith- Napoleon Hill explained, "The mind has no limitations except those which conflict with the laws of nature." Think and act as if you already have what you want in life, and you'll increase your chances of success dramatically. What are some limiting beliefs that don't serve any beneficial purpose for you that you need to let go of? Ask yourself this: what do you have to believe in reaching the next level in your life?

5 Learning from Adversity and Defeat– According to Napoleon Hill, "Often, opportunities come disguised in the form of misfortune or temporary defeat." In other words, use adversity and defeat as nothing more than lessons to learn from and signals that you need to change your plans. When you experience a setback, think about the new pathways to success opening to you due to your unique life circumstances. Here's another quote that's pertinent to this law: "Look for the seed of an equivalent benefit in every failure." In other words, try to think from the mindset that life happens for you, not to you.

6 Pleasing Personality– this is the habit of being generally respectful and friendly with people. This law doesn't suggest being a people pleaser and a pushover. But, if you want to achieve great things in life, you'll most likely need to build relationships with great achievers who are further along in the journey toward your goals than you are. And to build relationships with those people, they need to enjoy being around you.

7 Personal Initiative — This is one of the most important habits you need to be a successful entrepreneur or leader. This is the habit of starting activities that are important to you and seeing them through to completion. If something critical needs to be resolved, don't wait for permission or external validation to do it.

8 Creative Vision — This habit mentally visualizes what you want most and the actions to help you acquire them. Napoleon Hill stated, "All achievements, all earned riches, have their beginning in an idea."

9 Positive Mental Attitude — This is the habit of looking for every situation in life's positive side, especially during failure and adversity. And when we start to feel negative emotions, we must learn to change our mindsets to pursue our goals with a clear mind.

10 Enthusiasm — This is the habit of keeping yourself energized by focusing your life on what you love most. It would be best to have confidence and a high energy level to reach your goals when you encounter setbacks.

11 Self-Discipline — This is the habit of avoiding negative choices that will cost you more than you gain. This one might be a little subjective, but in general, avoid bad habits that could take you off track from your goals.

12 Accurate Thinking — This is the habit of making decisions and forming opinions based on information and tangible evidence. Try to avoid biases and assumptions that could cause you to make bad decisions.

13 Controlled Attention — This is the habit of prioritizing your time and energy to stay focused on the most important and beneficial. If you work full-time and build a side business, you will need controlled attention to spend at least 20 — 40 hours a week toward building that business.

14 Teamwork — this involves coordinating with others to work toward a common goal. The bigger and more ambitious your dream, the more talented people you'll need to help you reach it.

15 Maintenance of Sound Health — this is the habit of keeping your energy level up by eating healthy food and exercising regularly.

16 Budgeting of Time and Money—this is the habit of taking time every day to move closer to your definite primary purpose and saving and investing money to ensure that your finances steadily grow.

17 Establishing Positive Habits involve repeating desirable thought patterns and behaviors until they become effortless and self-moving.

PERSONAL LAWS

They all identify with the makeup of use and understanding of the components of the mind.

(1.) Conscious. (2.) Subconscious and (3.) Ego. Understanding the three processes opens the doors to all enlightenment; they are subject to a core belief system and law programs by default. Everything is housed in the framework of our skull; our brains must be protected and well-hydrated; it is where the mind resides and is central to everything we do. We are 3 part beings, inescapable.

These originated from the laws as if you were a public corporation; they determine the actions of any event you are willing to approach personally. These rules are a self-imposed badge of honor and respect based on learned experiences and, If any, affirmations; they must be from the foundation of your belief.

An example is I will never have a physical relationship with my best friend's spouse, even if the spouse was to die. Instead, I would always treasure my friends' relationship by being the best friend to their spouse in support as possible.

- I will never mistreat our friendship by secretly plotting against them. I will not cheat anyone for a profit nor make false claims to get the edge over a friend that trusts in me.

- I will not steal from anyone or take what does not belong to me.

- I will avoid gossip about anyone and will not spread rumors about people to fit in a group.

- I will not hate someone because of their race or heritage.

- I will not hold others, hostage for the sins of others, no matter what happens.

- I will not rehash the hateful past of abuse, racism in history to rekindle negative emotions.

- I will not judge a man or woman who begs on the street, and I do not know their struggle.

- I will not pray for someone suffering without helping as best I can if I can.

These are the things that I use, and there are other examples.

UNDERSTANDING VALUE

Words are physical Assets,

Your words are more valuable than gold, platinum, silver, diamonds, crude oil, and even the national treasury. They are the only absolute security and Commodity you possess.

All the power to execute a trade is in you. You and you alone can make it happen. If you are waiting on God to

come and do it, it's not going to happen. God rested and gave the authority to Adam, and that same authority rests on you and me. Adam had his assignment and blew it. After Noah, the same old thing continues.

God spoke to the prophets, delivering the message to the people, and man continues the sin even more today. So, God said, let us make man in our image. He was not talking about a fleshly body image either; he spoke of his appearance, the Spirit. Jesus was the plan of redemption for God to reclaim what belongs to him, "YOU," but he does not interfere with your "Will." When Adam fell out of the image, the act of being born again puts us back in the image. This was the purpose of Jesus.

Everything you want in life is in your hands. You are the manager, and you are the one in charge. God is a creator. He is not a manager; he will bless the labor of your hands. God has given you everything you and I need to succeed in life. He is alive inside the believer that received him. Just do it until you get it done. Stop waiting!!! My prayer every day is Lord gives me the strength to do what I must do.

"THE ONLY TWO THINGS YOU TRULY OWN IN THIS LIFE ARE YOUR MIND AND YOUR TIME; BEST YOU LEARN HOW TO USE THEM IN FAITH."

SEALED UNTO THE DAY OF REDEMPTION

Sealed unto redemption is the benefit of accepting Jesus Christ, regardless of your status in life through divine substance you have of a place of permanence. The failure of religious institutions to understand the matters of the spirit concerning spiritual things is revealed. Instead of turning out seminary students for ministerial credentials, students graduate in academics. They do not understand the power of the living God and the Holy Spirit that dwells in you upon accepting Jesus. We have been taught wrong for a lifetime. The total embodiment of the Holy Spirit comes to live in you, and acknowledging its presence unleashes the full power of God in you; too many, this remains a mystery.

True discernment comes from the Faith that he is alive in you. Without Faith, you cannot begin your journey of purpose, whatever it is. Holiness and power from the Spirit, which by design accelerate expectancy in knowing it's all true and settled in your consciousness the very hope of what you desire.

He stated that if you come to me, I would, at no wise, cast out anyone that comes to me; therefore, ministers teach that he will accept you as you are and rightly so because it is true.

John 6:36-38

Amplified Bible

36 But as I told you, you have seen Me, and still, you do not believe. 37 All that My Father gives Me will come to Me; and the one who comes to Me I will most certainly not cast out [I will never, never reject anyone who follows Me]. 38 For I have come down from heaven, not to do My own will, but to do the will of Him who sent Me.

This blessing comes because God is not a man and cannot lie. He plainly says that man has the form of Godliness but denies the power thereof. They look religious and full of faith but only in word, not understanding the word.

So, he believes the words in a vague sense, but not in the physical. Thus, never fully accepting the power of God through the impartation of the Spirit. What doubting Thomas showed by the requesting to see and touch as a condition of his faith shows his lack of faith. But Jesus said how much GREATER it would be if he could believe without seeing and touching his wounds.

John 20:25

Amplified Bible

The King James Version of the Bible is translated as: The other disciples, therefore, said unto him, we have seen the Lord. But he said unto them, Except I shall see the print of the nails in his hands, put my finger into the mark of the nails, and thrust my hand into his side; I will not believe.

John 20:27

Amplified Bible

Then He said to Thomas, "Reach here with your finger, and see My hands; and put out your hand and place it in My side. Do not be unbelieving, but [stop doubting and] believe."

John 20:29

Amplified Bible

Jesus said to him, "Because you have seen Me, do you now believe? So blessed [happy, spiritually secure, and favored by God] are they who did not see [Me] and yet believed [in Me]."

These statements are genuine and authentic; blessed are the poor in spirit, for theirs is the kingdom of Heaven.

The Physical is precisely what God's word is; everything made beginning from his word originated from the Mouth of God Himself.

John 1:1

Amplified Bible

In the beginning [before all time] was the Word (Christ), the Word was with God, and the Word was God Himself.

John 1:14

Amplified Bible

The Word Made Flesh

14 And the Word (Christ) became flesh and lived among us, and we [actually] saw His glory, glory as belongs to the [One and] only begotten Son of the Father, [the truly unique Son, the only one of His kind, who is] full of grace and truth (free of deception).

So, these are the poor in spirit, but God's mercy and grace plan are unchanging and sealed. This is the social security of heavenly assurance. But they lack the real power of the spirit.

Some confuse this as if Jesus is talking about the poor; he was not. He states the poor will always be with you, but I'm only here a little while. Jesus said that the poor would always be with you; being poor is not a prerequisite of salvation, nor does being poor get you closer to heaven. Poverty is a curse because, in God, you are rich. Gold miners stake their claim, so stake yours in the riches in Faith in Jesus.

Jesus said, Let the poor say they are rich and the weak say they are strong. How can we be in God and have lack in our life? You don't' understand how the Comforter works in your life, and you don't recognize who or what he is to you. Trust in Jesus and know that he is God and receive the benefits of what is available.

Good Health and Life:

There is only one thing for sure guaranteed to every one of us, and that is death. It is a self-fulfilling prophecy. Worrying about a future event serves no purpose; it is just an event we build into our living. As we understand the nature of the event, we can find peace with the prospect of living and slow the process of dying. Creation is based on the belief that you are the fruit of the garden. Just as everything else on the planet has a life cycle, we are no different. Understanding what and who you are lessens the negotiation process of something you can only manage unto completion.

The benefit of knowing is how to contend with managing the house you live in, which is the body. Knowing that helps you understand the nature of the occasion. If you have ever grown a plant or a garden, everything needs its environment to sustain itself. The very least of them is water. The reality is, good health is "priceless." But for us to help in the deterioration of the body is disturbing. If you believe you were created from the dirt, it is easy to assume what's in the soil is good. When my wife became ill, she was diagnosed and given one day to 10 days to live. I did not accept that, so I spoke aloud from my Spirit in Faith, and God heard me.

I immediately found everything close to the earth in natural medicine and mega-dose her on every front. As the doctors had said, they couldn't do anything. I looked under her feet; there was no expiration date, so I ignored the doctors. In a short period, she had lost sixty-six pounds. It wasn't enjoyable to see her in such a state. I just kept seeing her whole and healthy, and nine years later, she is still alive and not using the oxygen tanks provided to her with several college degrees and gained all her weight back in short order using healthy fat.

Over time she has exercised her Faith to sustain a healthy living through a fixed mindset. Knowing for sure who lives inside her helps understand the proper engagement of the Spirit. The Spirit cannot be sick, cannot be weak, cannot be lacking. We have authority and should possess spiritual weapons against poverty, sickness, and diseases as a believer.

If you can trust in God, let him be true and every man a liar. Believe what the Bible says about Jesus inside you. You have broken the curse of 95% of the Christian's unbelief. Our action of Faith supercharges miracles and blessings. The replicating counter is the Universal axis, and Spiritual life responds according to your efforts when requests have been made on a standing truth. Instead, you accept and believe that Faith will be your validation of his promises because his existence is immovable. So let his "Word" be alive, and his truth be told. We are the managers of all creation, be in charge.

When I see people of faith suffering in sickness, poverty, and lack, I say let the building crumble; they are houses of merchandise, businesses of religion, rather than a temple of Faith. Weak and useless without the power of God. They are teaching lukewarm sermons of compromise that has made the power of God to no effect. Jesus brought us power through faith and the Comforter.

It seems that everyone is looking for something mystical or a magic bullet to solve problems, or as I call them, situations.

People are constantly seeking the mysterious for something new to give themselves feelings of empowerment and self-worth outside of the embodiment of the comforter.

These emotions to want to feel different, see something different are the driving forces behind all change. Everything else is secondary. We seek self-worth in the values of the masses' opinions and find ourselves following cults of all types and participating in satanic rituals and poison politics.

When we are entirely able to handle whatever comes our way.

CHAPTER 9

THE BIBLES AND TIMELINES

Timeline from Adam until Christ chronologically ordered

The chronology is from the first edition of the King James Version of the Bible, printed by Philadelphia printer Matthew Carey in 1801. The Timeline mainly This text is a sequel to Rev. James Ussher's 1658 book Annals of the World. According to Ussher's chronology, the world's history was divided into six ages, beginning with creation and ending with the fall of Jerusalem. Carey's Bible mentions the First Age, but it does not mention subsequent periods. Despite this, "from" clearly marks each age's beginning. So it is proved by the Scriptures, from the Collection of diverse Authors.

(As an Author of the Master Managers Handbook, I cannot verify any proven statements 100 percent because the believer gives respect and authority to the word. Wicked men can easily manipulate and control others for their selfish motives. In my opinion, let God lead you in your understanding. You must believe in something to have hope. My belief is in The Son of God.)

An example of this truth is the Slave Bible, on display at the national museum. Currently on display at the Museum of the Bible in Washington, DC., is a special exhibition dedicated to the use of a rare Bible during the 1800s to convert and educate slaves.

This Bible is noteworthy not just because of its rarity but also because of its content, or rather, lack thereof. Naturally, therefore, texts that might inspire rebellion or liberation are excluded.

So, as you can see, people use religion as an end to a purpose.

UNDERSTANDING BC AND AD

What is the real meaning?
Clarification

When we think of B.C. and A.D., commonly believed that it stands for "before Christ" and AD stands for "after death." There is only half of an assumption that is true. It's hard to imagine how 1 B.C. Was "before Christ" and "before Antioch" 1 "after death"? British Columbia A.D. stands for "before Christ." It means "in the year of our Lord" in Latin." The B.C./A.D. The dating system is scripturally inclusive in the Bible. Unfortunately, it was not fully implemented and accepted until several centuries after Jesus' death.

These are the timelines given by Scholars, Priest, Bishops, Cardinals, Evangelists, and Ministers worldwide. So about 6000 years from Adam to Now.

TIMELINES

Three thousand nine hundred seventy-four years, six months, and ten days since Adam until Christ; from the birth of Christ, unto this present year, is 1801. So then the whole sum and number of years from the beginning of the world unto the

124

current year of our Lord God 1801 are 5775 years, six months, and the said odd ten days. (This is not my personal opinion, it's the Spiritual leaders we had chosen to govern our Spiritual lives when the Comforter came to fulfill this duty; we are the managers, just as Adam's authority.

SOME OF THE BIBLES

Let's look at all the bibles and where they come from:

10. The Bishop's Bible
Publish Date: 1568
Language: English
Printer/Writer/Translator: Church of English Bishops
Discovery or Publish Location: England
The Bishop's Bible photo source: Wikimedia Commons

Immediately before Elizabeth I of England, her half-sister, Queen Mary, known as "Bloody Mary," banned the Bible from England. However, when Elizabeth took the throne, she immediately reinstated it and asked the Archbishop of Canterbury, Matthew Parker, to develop a new book version, "The Bishop's Bible."

The Bishop's Bible was fewer than ten bishops translated on three earlier versions: Greek, Latin, and Hebrew. Unfortunately, there are several errors in the language, and though it's possible to find it, it's seldom reprinted today.

9. The Geneva Bible
Publish Date: 1560
Language: English
Printer/Writer/Translator: William Tyndale and Myles Coverdale
Discovery or Publish Location: Geneva, Switzerland
The Geneva Bible photo source: Wikimedia Commons

Geneva, Switzerland, is where the Geneva Bible was created in 1560. The Bible was, however, in English. Theologians from England fled overseas during the reign of Queen Mary to continue their religious studies. This migration resulted in the creation of the Geneva Bible. Translated mainly by William Tyndale, with help from Myles Coverdale, the Bible is one of the most significant in Christian history. The Pilgrims brought it to America on the Mayflower after a long direct translation that lasted many years. Moreover, the Geneva Bible was the first mass-produced mechanically printed Bible. The Geneva Bible is still available today.

8. The Great Bible
Publish Date: 1539
Language: Modern English
Printer/Writer/Translator: Myles Coverdale
Discovery or Publish Location: England
The Great Bible photo source: Wikimedia Commons

King Henry VIII of England commissioned the Great Bible. The King requires every parish in the country to buy a copy of this Bible from the Crown. There were six complete editions of the Great Bible, and somebody made more than 9,000 copies.

During this time, the only version read of the Bible was allowed in English churches. So great Bible was more of a parallel to Tyndale Bible, a Bible that wasn't. The texts in this book were written by William Tyndale and are a combination of Biblical texts. It was also the first Bible with a title page with color.

7. The Coverdale Bible
Publish Date: 1535
Language: Modern English
Printer/Writer/Translator: Compiled by Myles Coverdale
Discovery or Publish Location: Zurich, Switzerland or Antwerp, Belgium
The Coverdale Bible photo source: Wikimedia Commons

Coverdale's Bible was the first translation of the entire Bible in Modern English, including both Old and New Testaments. At least 20 editions of the Coverdale Bible were published, including the final edition published in 1553.

The man who created the Coverdale Bible was one of the most exciting things about it. The man's name was Myles Coverdale, and he worked as a Bible printer.

6. The Leningrad Codex
Publish Date: 1008 AD
Language: Hebrew
Printer/Writer/Translator: Samuel ben Jacob and Others
Discovery or Publish Location: Cairo, Egypt
The Leningrad Codex photo source: Wikimedia Commons

As the oldest complete Hebrew translation of the Bible, the Leningrad Codex is known for its age. The Leningrad Codex is significant historically and religiously and one of the best examples of Jewish medieval art. The manuscript also shows that the Old Testament of the Bible has hardly changed in thousands of years. One unusual thing about the Leningrad Codex is that some books are out of order compared to the traditional Bible. However, despite its age, it remains in remarkable condition. The Leningrad Codex is on display at the National Library of Russia today.

5. The Aleppo Codex
Publish Date: 930 AD
Language: Hebrew
Printer/Writer/Translator: Masoretes
Discovery or Publish Location: Tiberias, Israel
The Aleppo codex photo source: Wikimedia Commons

A complete manuscript of the Bible can be found in the Aleppo Codex. For over 1,000 years, it was held and protected in Jewish communities in Egypt, Jerusalem, and Syria, hence its name. Finally, it was smuggled out of Syria In 1958 and given to Izhak Ben-Zvi, the President of Israel.

This manuscript is 294 pages long, but many missing pages are due to damage caused by a riot in 1947. The missing pages have been searched several times, but ultimately no one knows what happened — located now at the Israel Museum.

4. Codex Ephraemi Rescriptus
Publish Date: 460 AD
Language: Greek
Printer/Writer/Translator: Unknown Scribes
Discovery or Publish Location: Unknown, but Possibly Egypt
Codex Ephraemi Rescriptus photo source: Wikimedia Commons

Another ancient Bible is the Codex Ephraemi Rescriptus. In the past, most of the Old Testament was believed to be complete, but today only about two-thirds of the New Testament still exists. The name of the scribes may be unknown, but researchers believe that two writers wrote this document.

According to experts who have studied the Codex Ephraemi Rescriptus, those who wrote it on other manuscripts used the same content.

Because the scribe switched from one manuscript to another as he wrote, you can see the Codex Ephraemi Rescriptus in Paris today. Located at the Bibliothèque nationale de France.

3. Codex Alexandrinus
Publish Date: 400 to 440 AD
Language: Greek
Printer/Writer/Translator: Unknown Scribes
Discovery or Publish Location: Alexandria, Egypt — Gifted to King Charles I of England in 1627
Codex Alexandrinus photo source: Wikimedia Commons

One of the oldest Bibles in history is the Codex Alexandrinus. The British Library website offers a complete reproduction of the Bible, which is 773 pages long. It is handwritten on vellum.

As a result of its delicate nature, only its curators handle the Codex Alexandrinus.

Some scholars believe the Alexandrinus Codex to be among the world's best. Scholars also considered it to be the most complete New Testament version. As a result, we now have most of our New Testaments in this version.

2. Codex Sinaiticus (The Sinai Bible)
 Publish Date: 330 – 360 AD
Language: Greek
Printer/Writer/Translator: Unknown Scribes
Discovery or Publish Location: Saint Catherine's Monastery in the Sinai Peninsula
Codex Sinaiticus (The Sinai Bible) photo source: Wikimedia Commons

Until the oldest Bible was scientifically dated, the Codex Sinaiticus was considered the oldest Bible. Manuscripts were discovered in the 19th century, though they were incomplete. In London, the British Library displays most of these components.

Several parts of the Old Testament are missing when you look at the whole Codex Sinaiticus.

However, it accepted that initially, the whole Old Testament was part of the codex. Therefore, approximately half of the Old Testament remains, and the complete New Testament.

1. Codex Vaticanus (The Latin Bible)
Publish Date: 300-305 AD
Language: Greek
Printer/Writer/Translator: Unknown Scribes
Discovery or Publish Location: Unknown, but possibly Rome, Alexandria, or Caesarea

Codex Sinaiticus (The Sinai Bible) photo source: Wikimedia Commons the Codex Vaticanus was kept at the Vatican Library since around the 15th century. It is the oldest known Bible. Printed on vellum sheets, and they believed that at least three scribes translated them.

As it was written only a couple of hundred years after Jesus died, The Codex Vaticanus, according to most scholars, is the most accurate Bible currently available. Additionally, it is a very good translation of the Greek Bible. The Bible is remarkably intact and mostly complete, even though it is not a complete translation. It lacks most of Genesis, Hebrews, and Revelations, however.

Let us try and understand what these aspired men did in light of the word of God, given to the people of God. But, unfortunately, most of the beginning of the Bible is missing. Most of the example of your belief system of living by faith is missing and ends when we exit. Okay? This may explain why we do not fully understand how to engage the living God through the Comforter.

131

CHAPTER 10

MIRACLES

"Miracles are throughout the Bible with demonstrations from God with power and might. God stated that he is the same God as initially, and he does not change." Let's take a closer look at them and what do they mean. If God is your source, then you have the same power for manifestation.

JESUS HEALS AN OFFICIAL'S SON

John 4.

43 After two days, he left for Galilee. 44 (Now Jesus himself had pointed out that a prophet has no honor in his own country.) 45 When he arrived in Galilee, the Galileans welcomed him. They witnessed all he had done in Jerusalem at the Passover Festival, for they also had been there.

46 Once more, he visited Cana in Galilee, where he had turned the water into wine. And there was a particular royal official whose son lay sick at Capernaum. 47 When this man heard that Jesus had arrived in Galilee from Judea, he went to him and begged him to come and heal his son, who was close to death.

48 "Unless you people see signs and wonders," Jesus told him, "You will never believe."

49 The royal official said, "Sir, come down before my child dies."

50 "Go," Jesus replied, "your son will live."

The man took Jesus at his word and departed. 51 While he was still on the way, his servants met him with the news that his boy was living. 52 When he inquired as to the time when his son got better, they said to him, "Yesterday, at one in the afternoon, the fever left him."

53 Then the Father realized that this was the exact time at which Jesus had said to him, "Your son will live." So, he and his whole household believed.

54 This was the second sign Jesus performed after coming from Judea to Galilee.

HEALING ON THE SABBATH

John 5

New International Version

THE HEALING POOL

1. Sometime later, Jesus went up to Jerusalem for one of the Jewish festivals. 2 Now there is in Jerusalem near the Sheep Gate a pool, which in Aramaic is called Bethesda and surrounded by five covered colonnades. 3 Here, many disabled people used to lie—the blind, the lame, the paralyzed. 4 From time to time, an angel of the Lord would come down and stir the waters. After the Angel went, the first one into the pool after each disturbance would cure whatever disease they had. 5 One who was there had been an invalid for thirty-eight years. 6 When Jesus saw him lying there and learned that he had been in this condition for a long time, he asked him, "Do you want to get well?"

7 "Sir," the invalid replied, "I have no one to help me into the pool when the waters stirred. While I am trying to get in, someone else goes down ahead of me."

8 Then Jesus said to him, "Get up! Pick up your mat and walk." 9 At once, the man was cured; he picked up his mat and walked.

The day on which this took place was a Sabbath, ten, and so the Jewish leaders said to the man who has healed you, "It is the Sabbath; the law forbids you to carry your mat."

11 But he replied, "The man who made me well said to me, 'Pick up your mat and walk.'"

12 So they asked him, "Who is this fellow who told you to pick it up and walk?"

13 The man healed had no idea who it was, for Jesus had slipped away into the crowd that was there.

14 Later, Jesus found him at the temple and said to him, "See, you are well again. Stop sinning, or something worse may happen to you." 15 The man went away and told the Jewish leaders that it was Jesus who had made him well.

THE AUTHORITY OF THE SON

16 So, because Jesus was doing these things on the Sabbath, the Jewish leaders began to persecute him. 17 In his defense, Jesus said to them, "My Father is always at his work to this very day, and I too am working." 18 For this reason, they tried even more to kill him; not only was he breaking the

Sabbath, but he was even calling God his own Father, making himself equal with God.

19 Jesus gave them this answer: "Very truly I tell you, the Son can do nothing by himself; he can do just what he sees his Father doing because whatever the Father does, the Son also does. 20 For the Father loves the Son and shows him all he does. Yes, and he's going to show him even greater works than these so that you will be amazed. 21 For just as the Father raises the dead and gives them life, even so, the son gives life to whom he is pleased to provide it through. 22 Moreover, the father judges no one but has entrusted all judgment to the son, 23 that all may honor the Son just as they honor the father. Whoever does not honor the Son does not honor the Father who sent him.

24 "Very truly I tell you, whoever hears my word and believes him who sent me has eternal life and will not be judged but has crossed over from death to life. 25 Very truly, I tell you, a time is coming and has now come when the dead will hear the voice of the Son of God and those who hear will live. 26 For as the Father has life in himself, he has granted the son also life. 27 And he has given him authority to judge because he is the Son of Man.

28 "Do not be amazed at this, for a time is coming when all who are in their graves will hear his voice 29 and come out — those who have done what is good will rise to live, and those who have done what is evil will rise to be condemned. 30 By myself, I can do nothing; I judge only as I hear, and my judgment is just, for I seek not to please myself but him who sent me.

Testimonies About Jesus

31 *"If I testify about myself, my testimony is not valid. 32 There is another who testifies in my favor, and I know that his testimony about me is true.*

33 *"You have sent to John, and he has testified to the truth. 34 Not that I accept human testimony, but I mention that you may be saved. 35 John was a lamp that burned and gave light, and you chose for a time to enjoy his light.*

36 *"I have testimony weightier than that of John. For the works that the father has given me to finish—the very works that I am doing—testify that the father has sent me. 37 And the father who sent me has himself testified concerning me. Nevertheless, you have never heard his voice nor seen his form, 38 nor does his word dwell in you, for you do not believe the one he sent. 39 You study the Scriptures diligently because you think that in them you have eternal life. These are the very Scriptures that testify about me, 40 yet you refuse to come to me to have life.*

41 *"I do not accept glory from human beings, 42 but I know you. I know that you do not have a love of God in your hearts. 43 I have come in my father's name, and you do not accept me; but if someone else comes in his name, you will receive him. 44 How can you believe since you get glory from one another but do not seek the glory that comes from the only God?*

45 *"But do not think I will accuse you before the father. Your accuser is Moses, on whom your hopes are set. 46 If you believed Moses, you would believe me, for he wrote about me. 47 But since you do not believe what he wrote, how are you going to believe what I say?"*

BREAD OF LIFE

Jesus Feeds the Five Thousand

6 Sometime after this, Jesus crossed to the far shore of the Sea of Galilee (that is, the Sea of Tiberias), two and a great crowd of people followed him because they saw the signs he had performed by healing the sick. 3 Then Jesus went up on a mountainside and sat down with his disciples. 4 The Jewish Passover Festival was near.

5 When Jesus looked up and saw a great crowd coming toward him, he said to Philip, "Where shall we buy bread for these people to eat?" 6 He asked this only to test him, for he already had in mind what he was going to do.

7 Philip answered him, "It would take more than half a year's wages to buy enough bread for each one to have a bite!"

8 Another of his disciples, Andrew, Simon Peter's brother, spoke up, 9 "Here is a boy with five small barley loaves and two small fish, but how far will they go among so many?"

10 Jesus said, "Have the people sit down." There was plenty of grass there, and they sat down (about five thousand men were there). 11 Jesus then took the loaves, gave thanks, and distributed to those seated as much as they wanted. He did the same with the fish.

12 When they had all had enough to eat, he said to his disciples, "Gather the leftover pieces. Let nothing be wasted." 13 So they gathered them and filled twelve baskets with the pieces of the five barley loaves left over by those who had eaten.

14 After the people saw the sign Jesus performed, they began to say, "Surely this is the Prophet who is to come into the world." 15 Jesus, knowing that they intended to come and make him king by force, withdrew again to a mountain by himself.

JESUS WALKS ON THE WATER

16 When evening came, his disciples went down to the lake, 17 where they got into a boat and set off across the lake for Capernaum. By now, it was dark, and Jesus had not yet joined them. 18 A strong wind was blowing, and the waters grew rough. 19 When they had rowed about three or four miles, they saw Jesus approaching the boat, walking on water, and they were frightened. 20 But he said to them, "It is I; don't be afraid." 21 Then they were willing to take him into the boat, and immediately the boat reached the shore where they were heading.

22 The next day, the crowd that had stayed on the opposite shore of the lake realized that only one boat had been there and that Jesus had not entered it with his disciples but that they had gone away alone. 23 Then, some boats from Tiberias landed near the place where the people had eaten the bread after the Lord had given thanks. 24 Once the crowd realized that neither Jesus nor his disciples were there, they got into the boats and went to Capernaum, searching for Jesus.

JESUS IS THE BREAD OF LIFE

25 When they found him on the other side of the lake, they asked him, "Rabbi, when did you get here?"

26 Jesus answered, "Very truly I tell you, you are looking for me, not because you saw the signs, I performed but because you ate the loaves and had your fill. 27 Do not work for food that spoils, but for food that endures to eternal life, which the Son of Man will give you. For on him, God the Father has placed his seal of approval."

28 Then they asked him, "What must we do to do the works God requires?"

29 Jesus answered, "The work of God is this: to believe in the one he has sent."

30 So they asked him, "What sign then will you give that we may see it and believe you? What will you do? 31 Our ancestors ate the manna in the wilderness; as it is written: 'He gave them bread from heaven to eat.'

32 Jesus said to them, "Very truly I tell you, it is not Moses who has given you the bread from heaven, but it is my Father who gives you the true bread from heaven. 33 For the bread of God is the bread that comes down from heaven and gives life to the world."

34 "Sir," they said, "always give us this bread."

35 Then Jesus declared, "I am the bread of life. Whoever comes to me will never go hungry, and whoever believes in me will never be thirsty. 36 But as I told you, you have seen me, and still, you do not believe. 37 All those the Father gives me will come to me, and whoever comes to me, I will never drive away. 38 For I have come down from heaven not to do my will but to do the will of him who sent me. 39 And this is the will of him who sent me, that I shall lose none of all those he has given me but raise them at the last day. 40 For my father's will is that everyone who looks to the Son and believes in him shall have eternal life, and I will raise them at the last day."

41 At this, the Jews there began to grumble about him because he said, "I am the bread that came down from heaven." 42 They said, "Is this not Jesus, the Son of Joseph, whose father and mother we know? How can he now say, 'I came down from heaven?'"

43 "Stop grumbling among yourselves," Jesus answered. 44 "No one can come to me unless the Father who sent me draws them, and I will raise them at the last day. 45 <u>It is written in the Prophets: 'They will all be taught by God.</u>' Therefore, everyone who has heard the Father and learned from him comes to me. 46 No one has seen the Father except the One from God; only he has seen the Father. 47 Very truly, I tell you, the one who believes has eternal life. 48 I am the bread of life. 49 Your ancestors ate the manna in the wilderness, yet they died. 50 But here is the bread that comes down from heaven, which anyone may eat and not die. 51 I am the living bread that came down from heaven. Whoever eats this bread will live forever. This bread is my flesh, which I will give for the life of the world."

52 Then the Jews began to argue sharply among themselves, "How can this man give us his flesh to eat?"

53 Jesus said to them, "Very truly I tell you, unless you eat the flesh of the Son of Man and drink his blood, you have no life in you. 54 Whoever eats my flesh and drinks my blood has eternal life, and I will raise them at the last day. 55 For my flesh is real food, and my blood is real drink. 56 Whoever eats my flesh and drinks my blood remains in me, and I in them. 57 Just as the living Father sent me and I live because of the father, the one who feeds on me will live because of me. 58 This is the bread that came down from heaven. Your ancestors ate manna and died, but whoever feeds on this bread will live forever." 59 He said this while teaching in the synagogue in Capernaum.

MANY DISCIPLES DESERT JESUS

60 On hearing it, many of his disciples said, "This is a hard teaching. Who can accept it?"

61 Aware that his disciples were grumbling about this, Jesus said to them, "Does this offend you? 62 Then what if you see the Son of Man ascend to where he was before! 63 The Spirit gives life; the flesh counts for nothing. The words I have spoken to you—they are full of the Spirit and life. 64 Yet some of you do not believe." For Jesus had known from the beginning which of them did not believe and who would betray him. 65 He went on to say, "This is why I told you that no one could come to me unless the Father has enabled them."

66 From this time, many of his disciples turned back and no longer followed him.

67 "You do not want to leave too, do you?" Jesus asked the Twelve.

68 Simon Peter answered him, "Lord, to whom we shall go? You have the words of eternal life. 69 We have come to believe and to know that you are the Holy One of God."

70 Then Jesus replied, "Have I not chosen you, the Twelve? Yet one of you is a devil!" 71 (He meant Judas, the Son of Simon Iscariot, who, though one of the twelve, was later to betray him.)

CHAPTER 11

NATURAL DISASTERS

Floods, Tsunamis, hurricanes, Fire

I am appalled that the church has made God the destroyer of humanity; I can understand those who do not know God's authentic truth. Not everything we hear lines up with the spirit. The spirit bears witness to the fact. The secular community has seen the church walls come down and the cover withdrawn for all to see because it has predominantly become a fraud embedded in politics. It looks like they still need a King. Ministers must speak the truth, but churches have chosen parties over faith and compromise the reality in today's political climate. The power of God is rendered powerless because the proper interpretation of his word is not conveyed to the believers.

What happens to all the powers that God promise after the Holy Spirit was to come upon us? They are waiting on the receiver to accept and acknowledge. Everything that God promised he delivered, but the religious community looked for a whore to replace God. They found a home in commercialization and politics. Being socially submissive has destroyed the standing of the ministry. It has no power over anything except promoting podcasts, building buildings, and raising money.

With the millions of Rabbi's, Pastors, Ministers, Evangelists, Bishops, Cardinals, and the Pope, you would think that someone could stop this massive devastation. But, nope, they were all in hiding even when the pandemic came. They have no power. I can truthfully name over ten horrible conditions, several unto death, where God has healed me.

My faith in my God has always come through for my loved ones and me. So, trust in him, who I honor; he remembers his promises. God is and more than a prayer away; he is inside you through his Son Jesus Christ (the Comforter), the people who understand by revelation knowledge knows the spirit of God and where he resides.

The genuine faith is in your belief, I can't tell you who or what the name is, but mine is Jesus. I don't condemn anyone for what they believe. That's not my place to be your judge. A sign is if your faith doesn't work, change, and try Jesus Christ without religion; try him through faith.

Look at all the death and destruction left behind, not to include mass killings and suicides. How many died in fear and no hope because the church never taught the truth to them. So many had a religion but no real power — false hopes and false teaching, with no genuine standing faith in the authority of God in you. Just church rituals every Sunday, Saturday, or whatever day they worship. Even nations at war over religion. None of that is GOD! He is a God of peace, love, and compassion.

With the fatalities worldwide with Covid 19, I would suspect that many of these people thought the world was coming to an end. And to many, it was the end of the world because untold amounts of people died, and leaders with dictatorial attitudes caused an even greater mess. But, remember, we are the managers, not God. They were playing with the lives of millions for the sake of politics. I cannot believe that humanity has suffered so greatly and still has not figured it out. Jesus said, without me, you can do nothing. Not understanding the position of the Holy Spirit is where most of us are apart.

John 15
King James Bible
Jesus the True Vine

1. I am the true vine, and my father is the husbandman. 2. Every branch in me that beareth not fruit he taketh away: and every branch that beareth fruit, he purgeth it, that it may bring forth more fruit. 3. Now ye are clean through the word which I have spoken unto you. 4. Abide in me, and I in you. As the branch cannot bear fruit of itself, except it abide in the vine; no more can ye, except ye abide in me. 5. I am the vine; ye are the branches: He that abideth in me, and I in him, the same bringeth forth much fruit: for without me ye can do nothing.

Because of false teaching and misinformation of engaging the Spirit of God, this nation has suffered, even this whole world.

Moses supposedly parted the Red Sea.

Then Moses stretched out his hand over the sea, and the Lord drove the sea back by a strong east wind all night and made the dry sea land, and the waters divided.

Exodus 14:21

After leading his people out of Egypt and to the "promised land" of Canaan, Moses received the Ten Commandments from God on Mount Sinai in the Bible and Quran. So, the question is, God gave one man all his authority to deliver his people, and all the clergy of today have nothing. God does not change. I think God is crying as loud today as before. "LET MY PEOPLE GO" from the hypocrisies of the religious cult-like following, political and commercial capitalism. The fact is God has already given you everything, but religions hide it for insidious reasons.

There were over 5000 individuals, including women and children, who were held in bondage for 400 years, about the same length of time as African Americans in America. (HUH) A mighty God could blow out of his nostrils and release his people. I wonder did any of them think about fighting.

Yet Samson took the jawbone of a donkey and killed 1,000 Philistine soldiers. Samson Kills 1,000 Philistines

When Samson[a] arrived at Lehi, the Philistines came shouting to meet him. The Spirit of the Lord rushed upon him, so the ropes bound him were as burned by fire, and his bonds dissolved. He happened upon a jawbone from a putrefying donkey, reached out to grab it, and killed 1,000 men with it. Then Samson declared,

Judges 15:14-16

MAJOR EVENTS IN THE HISTORY OF "A.D." ("I AM SURE MANY WERE PEOPLE OF FAITH AND ASK WHERE GOD WAS.")

Look at other examples of events by our scientists and archaeologist using technologies 60 years old, called radiocarbon dating.

We are supposed to believe something is dated billions of years old when no one has been around to verify or confirm any of it. We should be ashamed of being duped into following this kind of crazy outlandish material as facts. But might I be the first to say, impossible for any of them to know? You would be better off calling Macco painting for answers than listen to that foolishness. Might I add here science is excellent, but we must question this kind of data at some point?

What Happened in Brief:

According to abundant geological evidence, an asteroid roughly 10 km (6 miles) across hit Earth about 65 million years ago. This impact made a massive explosion and a crater about 180 km (approximately 110 miles) across. The explosion threw debris into the atmosphere, severely altering the climate and leading to the extinction of roughly 3/4 of species that existed, including the dinosaurs.

(This estimate is mind-blowing for any sane person to use. There is no way this person that made this estimate shouldn't be on meds.)

(In my opinion, I don't understand why a God that is infinite in time would start all this 6000 years ago. My faith, Jesus is the evidence of God, and God the evidence of Jesus, both God and Jesus the proof of the Holy Spirit. If you were to follow all the invalidated scenarios, you are on a bridge to nowhere.)

Let's LOOK AT THE TSUNAMI

When we see disasters from millions to thousands of people dying worldwide, it makes one wonder if it was all these people's time to die, just as religious groups will judge they were or claim that God decided to destroy these people. Without hesitation, God had nothing to do with it. They were natural disasters and diseases that could have been handled in a very different way. They did not deserve to die, end of the story. But, to them, it was the end of the world. Their life ended that day if they did not know Jesus and receive the Comforter, with you have no communication with God.

In 2004, the Boxing Day tsunami killed more than 230,000 people across 14 countries, making it the deadliest in history.

A 9.1-magnitude earthquake struck Sumatra at 7:59 am local time on December 26, 2004.

It lasted up to 10 minutes, vibrating the Earth up to a centimeter, and was the third-biggest earthquake ever recorded.

As a result, the Indian Ocean was flooded with water, unleashing a massive tsunami

Anatomy of a tsunami (Reuters)

- Waves hit Northern Sumatra and the Nicobar Islands 15 minutes after the earthquake.

- Scientists measured Waves of up to 30 meters as the tsunami swept through Aceh, the hardest-hit region of Indonesia.

147

- Waves reached Sri Lanka, India, and Thailand a couple of hours after the earthquake struck.

- Antarctica and North America felt the effects as well.

- **A tsunami on Boxing Day (2004) caused numerous deaths and severe damage.**

- As many as 168,000 people died in Indonesia in the tsunami

- In Sri Lanka, 35,000 people died. While 18,000 were killed in India and 8,000 deaths in Thailand.

- Hundreds also died in Africa.

- Thousands of foreign travelers died in the disaster, including 26 Australians; all but two died in Thailand.

There is something wrong with our hearts and mind to believe God planned this disaster.

Hurricane Katrina

Hurricane Katrina was a tropical cyclone that struck the southeastern United States in late August 2005. The hurricane and its aftermath claimed more than 1,800 lives, and it ranked as the costliest natural disaster in U.S. history.

Diseases

As human civilizations flourished, so did infectious diseases. With a large number of people living close together and animals in unhealthy conditions, disease thrived. The new infections also spread worldwide through overseas trade routes, resulting in the first global pandemic.

Here are five of the world's worst pandemics.

1. Plague of Justinian

Yersinia pestis, a fatal disease known as the plague, was responsible for three of the deadliest pandemics recorded in history.

Constantinople was struck by the Plague of Justinian. The Romans carried grain from Egypt, a newly conquered land, over the Mediterranean Sea in 541 CE. Unfortunately, black rats that ate the grain brought fleas carrying the plague along with them.

2. The Invention of Quarantine because of the Black Death–

The plague never really disappeared, and it killed recklessly when it returned 800 years later. The Black Death hit Europe in 1347, which claimed 200 million lives within four years. **The Great Plague of London**

London never really caught a break after the Black Death. The plague resurfaced roughly every ten years; 20 percent of the men, women, and children living in the British capital were killed.

Smallpox — A European Disease Ravages the New World

Smallpox was rampant in Europe, Asia, and Arabia for centuries, a persistent menace that killed three out of ten people infected.

The indigenous peoples of contemporary-day Mexico and the United States had zero natural protection from smallpox, and the virus killed them by the tens of millions.

Centuries later, smallpox became the first virus epidemic to be ended by a vaccine. In the late 18th-century, a British doctor named Edward Jenner discovered that milkmaids infected with a milder virus called cowpox seemed immune to smallpox. So, Jenner famously inoculated his gardener's 8-year-old son

Cholera — A Victory for Public Health Research

In the early- to mid-19th century, cholera ripped through England, murdering tens of thousands. A British doctor named John Snow suspected that the mysterious disease was transmitted through London's drinking water. At the time, the disease was thought to be spread by foul air or by "miasmas."

Snow acted like a scientific Sherlock Holmes, investigating hospital records and morgue reports to track the precise locations of deadly outbreaks. For example, he created a geographic chart of cholera deaths over ten days. He found a group of 500 deadly viruses encompassing the Broad Street pump, a famous city well for drinking water.

Floods

In June 1938, Chinese Nationalist troops deliberately destroyed several dikes on the Yellow River to thwart the Japanese. The Chinese hoped to block Japanese access to a railway and stymie their westward progress using scorched earth tactics. Instead, it was a catastrophe for the environment. Having been unleashed, the muddy river tumbled off course and flooded Henan, Anhui, and Jiangsu provinces in the country's center. An estimated 4 million people were relocated from their dwellings, and 800,000 died after the deluge continued unchecked.

The Grote Mandrenke resulted from a vicious North Sea upheaval that swept across Europe in January 1362. From

25,000 to 100,000 people drowned, 60 different parishes in Denmark were "swallowed by the salt sea." Elsewhere in the Low Countries, erosion from the flood permanently transformed the coastline and led to the disappearance of whole islands.

CHAPTER 12
HUMAN TRAGEDY

Human Tragedy and the beat go on; might I add murders. From Emmit Till to George Floyd, Rodney King. Dr. Martin L. King, Trayvon Martin, and the list are endless....

TO BE SOLD on board the Ship Bance-Island, on tuesday the 6th of May next, at Ashley-Ferry; a choice cargo of about 250 fine healthy NEGROES, just arrived from the Windward & Rice Coast. —The utmost care has already been taken, and shall be continued, to keep them free from the least danger of being infected with the SMALL-POX, no boat having been on board, and all other communication with people from Charles-Town prevented. Austin, Laurens, & Appleby.

N. B. Full one Half of the above Negroes have had the SMALL-POX in their own Country.

The Slave Bible

The Museum of the Bible in Washington, D.C., is a rare Bible from the 1800s used by British missionaries to convert, change and educate slaves.

What's notable about this Bible is not just its rarity but its content, or rather the lack of content. It excludes any portion of text that might inspire rebellion or liberation.

Anthony Schmidt, an assistant curator of Bible and Religion in America at the museum, says the first instance of this abridged version titled, Parts of the Holy Bible, selected for the use of the Negro Slaves, in the British West-India Islands, was published in 1807.

As people come from various backgrounds, Anthony Schmidt of the Museum of the Bible says that encountering the Bible can vary significantly from person to person.

"About 90 percent of the Old Testament is missing [and] 50 percent of the New Testament is missing," Schmidt says. "Put in another way, there are 1,189 chapters in a standard protestant Bible. But unfortunately, this Bible contains only 232."

Schmidt says passages that could have prompted rebellion were removed, for example:

"There is neither Jew nor Greek; there is neither bond nor free, there is neither male nor female: for ye is all one in Christ Jesus." Galatians 3:28

Galatians 3:27-29

27 For all of you baptized into Christ have clothed yourselves with Christ. 28 There is neither Jew nor Greek, slave nor free, male nor female, for you are all one in Christ Jesus. 29 And if you belong to Christ, then you are Abraham's seed and heirs according to the promise....

How can we resolve this seeming contradiction?

In Genesis 15:13, God told Abram that his descendants would be slaves in a foreign land for 400 years. (Acts 7:6)

¹⁹ God is not a man that he should lie; neither the son of man, that he should repent: hath he said, and shall he not do it? Or hath he spoken, and shall he not make it good?

Numbers 23:19

From the beginning, God the Father and Jesus are one with the Holy Spirit. We are all Descendants of Abraham, and the scripture says.

They answered him, we are Abraham's seed, and were never in bondage to any man: how sayest thou, Ye shall be made are free?

John 8:33 KJV

Jesus Christ is the same yesterday, and today, and forever.

Hebrews 13:8 KJV

"He does not change, but religion has been the most destructive force for people of Christianity."

Abraham's Promise: The promises God made to Abraham are astounding. Based upon Abraham's faith and obedience, God, said, *"I will make you a great nation; I will bless you and make your name great, and you shall be a blessing. I will bless those who bless you, and I will curse him who curses you, and in you, all the families of the earth shall be blessed"* (Genesis 12:2-3).

From this foundational conversation between God and Abraham, the blessings poured on this man's descendants have been enormous. Ranging from land to countless descendants, to natural resources, to strategic gates of commerce, to military strength, the recipients of these God-given blessings have enjoyed a standard of living and prominence far above many other nations (Genesis 12:7; 22:17; 49:24-26).

On the contrary, the Bible teaches that salvation is open to all who heed God's call to repent their sins and receive the Holy Spirit.

FORM OF GODLINESS: It is truly unique how so many men of God can make beautiful expressions of the knowledge of Faith but rarely understand what true Faith is or how to accept the living spirit of God inside of them. Jesus states it so clearly.

2 Timothy 3:5-7

5 Having a form of godliness but denying the power thereof: from such turn away.

6 For of this sort are they which creep into houses, and lead silly captive women laden with sins, led away with divers lusts,

7 Ever learning, and never able to come to the knowledge of the truth.

Numbers 23:19

19 God is not human; he should lie, not a human being, and change his mind. Does he speak and then not act? Does he promise and not fulfill?

Parts of the Holy Bible, Selected for the
Use of the Negro Slaves, in the British
West-India Islands.
London: Law and Gilbert
1808

On Loan Courtesy of Fisk University, John Hope and Aurelia E.
Franklin Library, Special Collections, Nashville, Tennessee

SELECT PARTS

OF THE

HOLY BIBLE,

FOR THE USE OF THE

NEGRO SLAVES,

IN THE

BRITISH WEST-INDIA ISLANDS.

London:
PRINTED BY LAW AND GILBERT,
St. John's Square, Clerkenwell.
1807.

A little history on slavery. The bible notes God created Adam and Eve and told Adam to work and tend the garden. He did not make the third man a slave. This corrupt practice was all the lust of man to pursue power over another human he perceived as weak. It seems to me President Joe Biden has taken the same actions as Abraham Lincoln and leading the charge as Moses. It is fair to say he is a unique President with a passion for equal rights once held in question. His courageous action of choosing a multi-Racial woman vice president, making a federal holiday that marked the end of slavery, and not to mention crime bills for equal justice. All these things are righteous.

EGYPT400 PLUS YEARS OF SLAVERY

Genesis 15:13
English Standard Version

13 Then the Lord said to Abram, "Know for sure that your offspring will be sojourners in a land that is not theirs and will be servants there, and they be will slaves for four hundred years.

Hard to imagine for about 430 years that God's people were in captivity; 5000 men do not include women and children.

After the tenth plague, which slew the firstborn of every living thing in Egypt except those Israelites whose homes were marked by the blood of an innocent lamb, Pharaoh finally freed Israel. Pharaoh said to Moses, "Rise, go away from my people, both you and the Israelites! Go, worship the Lord, as you said. Take your flocks and your herds, as you said, and be gone." (Ex12:31-32)

In modern times of this generation, I find it hard to digest this event so easily, knowing that God would allow his people or any people of his creation to be in bondage or enslaved to anyone. When I think of Samson's story, killing 1000 Soldiers with the Jawbone of an Ass. And he was alone; it is hard to believe 5000 men could not fight, especially since they were making bricks. Sadly, I see the same correlations to our demise today as in the times of the Israelites unbelief in the power of God and are forced to suffer, just as we did with the coronavirus through the ignorance of our leaders and foolish pride.

After he came, he plainly said that ye should receive power after the Holy Spirit has come upon you. The problem of this generation is they cannot accept the fact that God himself has come into you as a spirit. They expect the mystery, a magic illusion of some type, simply because they do not go through any physical changes or feel something omnipresent; they discount the power of Faith.

The Promise of the Holy Spirit

(John 14:15–26)

5 Now, however, I am going to Him who sent Me; yet none of you asks Me, 'Where are You going?'

6 Instead, your hearts are filled with sorrow because I have told you these things. 7 But I tell you the truth, it is for your benefit that I am going away. Except If I go not away, the Holy Spirit will not come to you; but if I go, I will send Him to you.

8 And when He comes, He will convict the world regarding sin and righteousness and judgment: 9 regarding sin, because they do not believe in Me; 10 regarding morality, because I am going to the Father and you will no longer see Me; 11 and regarding judgment, because the prince of this world has been judged already. (This is because of his rebellion against God, reprobate mind, and un-repented nature.)

12 I still have much to tell you, but you cannot yet bear to hear it. 13 But, when the Spirit of truth comes, He will guide you into all truth. For He will not speak on His own, but He will speak what He hears, and He will declare to you what is to come. 14 He will glorify Me by taking from what is Mine and disclosing it to you. 15 Everything that belongs to the Father is Mine. That is why I said that the "Spirit" would be taken from whatever it is Mine and disclose it to you.

16 In a bit of time, you will be able to see Me no more, and then later you will see Me.

RADIOCARBON DATING

When I hear someone speak on carbon dating, I get sick because it is an unproven science developed in the same area of our modern technology today. Like a time warp sphere hole open, aliens approved this science to glimpse how man manipulated our brains by sowing misinformation in alternative realities. At some point, you would think someone would stand up and say stop the insanity. But unfortunately, we don't believe so.

To be precise, science is the most powerful tool to verify, research, and confirm what we don't know enough about or understand. But when we get into millions and billions of years, it is all nonsense, basically because no one on the planet or any galaxy has been around for thousands of years to validate any claims. No one can know what a hundred thousand years look like in the true and physical. So one cannot prove this is valid when we make these outlandish claims that cannot be confirmed.

Radiocarbon dating

As with carbon-14, radiocarbon dating uses the properties of radiocarbon, a radioactive carbon isotope, to determine an object's age from organic material. The technique was developed in the late 1940s at the University of Chicago by Willard Libby. He also received the Nobel Prize in Chemistry for his work in 1960.

The fact is that there is radiocarbon (14 C) in the Earth's atmosphere by the interaction of cosmic rays with atmospheric nitrogen; this is created constantly. As with carbon-14, radiocarbon dating uses the properties of radiocarbon, a radioactive carbon isotope, to determine an object's age from organic material.

In the case of dead plants or animals, the amount of 14 C in a fragment of wood or bone allows determining when the plant or animal died. The older a sample is, the fewer 14 C there is to be detected, and because the half-life of 14 C (the period after which half of a given piece will have decayed) is about 5,730 years, the oldest date reliably measured by this process dates to approximately 50,000 years ago. However, unique preparation methods occasionally make an accurate analysis of older samples possible.

CHAPTER 13

TECHNOLOGY TODAY

L et's look at technologies created in the last 400 years or so. Just the thought of all the generations of people with precisely the same circumstances and access over thousands, how did we get it right? Everything that exists comes from these three sources and nowhere else: water, air, and dirt. Yet, we spend too much time researching and offering an unverifiable opinion of human development and advancements. Are we preserving history or just a commercialized money pit baked up of lies?

Just imagine thousands of years of humans on the earth; I cannot believe we are the only ones with the intelligence to create everything from the same three elements. What's baffling is in Egypt, they have stones weighing thousands of tons, sitting over doorways, for the like of modern civilization and technology, we have no answer as to how they accomplished this feat? Even today, we still don't even have cranes that can lift this kind of weight, not to mention stones of similar weight raised to the top of Egyptian pyramids.

Look at what we accomplished in the last 400 years; accepting archaeologists and science's findings and dating systems if we wanted to play with reality. It's the same as sheep being led to the slaughterhouse. You must think. Nobody has all the answers, nobody is 100%, and nobody can live or die for you. So, live your best life and be empowered with your core belief system, and manage your life which is your duty.

- Wright brothers invented a plane in 1906

- The inventor of the locomotive train was Richard Trevithick 1804

- Martin Cooper invented mobile phones in 1973

- Charles Babbage invented the computer in 1821

- Gutenberg invented the printing press in the 15th century

- Rob Stothard invented smartphones in 1992

- Internet was invented in 1983 by Robert E Kah and Vin Cerf

- Thomas Edison created the light bulb in 1879. Lewis Howard Latimer is known for patenting the light bulb and the telephone.

- The inventor of TV was John Logie Baird; he also created color TV in 1926

- Elisha Atis invented the elevator in 1811

- Guillermo Marconi invented the radio in 1895

- James Watt invented the first engine in 1908

- Henry Ford Invented the car in 1908

- Henry W Seeley invented the electric iron in 1822

- Larry Page and Sergey created Google in 1998

- Horace Mann created the first school in 1796

- Richard Jordan Gatling invented the Gatling gun in 1892

- Alva J Fisher invented the washing machine in 1908

- Martin Cooper invented mobile phones in 1973

- J Ross Moore created a dryer in 1800

- Josephine Cochrane invented the dishwasher in 1886

- Sir John Harington invented the first commode in 1596. The first outhouse toilet designed was called a "privy." But, first, collection system around 4500 B.C. (I can assure you it was the caveman)

- Robert Hutchings Goddard invented the first liquid-fueled rocket. March 16, 1926

- Axel Cappelen's first heart surgery on the heart itself. Sept 4, 1895

- Dale Hale Williams, an African American, performed the first documented successful pericardium surgery in 1893

- First Psychological Researcher, Sigmund Freud 1856-1939, developed a topographical model of the mind.

- Alexander Fleming discovered penicillin in 1929

- Alessandro Volta invented the first electric battery with continuous power in 1799-1800 and discovered Methane.

LET'S TAKE A REAL LOOK INSIDE OF WHO DID WHAT:

Multiple inventors discovered electricity, but Benjamin Franklin got the credit.

Other contributors: Michael Faraday, Nikola Tesla, Thomas Edison, Joseph Swan, and many others.

Who Discovered Electricity?

Electricity is an energy that occurs naturally. However, many misconceptions abound about who discovered it. While Benjamin Franklin's experiments are often attributed to discovering electricity, they helped establish only the link between lightning and electricity, nothing else. Electricity was found in a way that is more complex than a man flying a kite. The concept of static electricity dates back over two thousand years ago. In about 600 BC, the Ancient Greeks discovered that rubbing fur on amber (fossilized tree resin) caused an attraction between the two.

Moreover, researchers and archaeologists in the 1930s discovered pots with copper sheets inside that might have been ancient batteries that produced light at ancient Roman sites. A similar device was found near Baghdad, which suggests that ancient Persians were also using batteries at that time. In 1600, William Gilbert, an English physician, used the Latin word "electricus" to describe certain substances' force when rubbed against each other. Positive and negative flows and early generators also were in the 17th century.

Who Discovered Electricity

Ben Franklin, In 1752, conducted his experimentation with a kite, a key, and a storm. He proved that lightning and tiny electric sparks were the same things.

Italian physicist Alessandro Volta discovered that chemical reactions could produce electricity, and in 1800 he constructed the voltaic pile (an early electric battery) that made a steady electric current. So, he was the first person to create a steady flow of electrical charge. Volta also developed the first electricity transmission by linking positively charged and negatively charged connectors and driving an electrical voltage.

In 1831 electricity became viable for use in technology when Michael Faraday created the electric dynamo (a crude power generator), which solved the problem of generating an electric current in an ongoing and practical way. The wire.

The British inventor Swan and Edison later collaborated to produce the first practical filament lamp. Edison used his direct-current system (DC) to illuminate the first New York electric street lamps in 1882.

Later, American inventor and industrialist George Westinghouse purchased and developed Tesla's patented motor for generating alternating current. The work of Westinghouse, Tesla, and others gradually convinced American society that the future of electricity lay with AC rather than DC.

And so, it was not just one person who discovered electricity. While electricity was known for thousands of years, several great minds worked on the problem to complete the concept when developing it commercially and scientifically.

"THIS IS A LIST OF TOP ACHIEVERS WITH A SINGLENESS OF PURPOSE THAT LEARNED HOW TO THINK"

Napoleon Hills researches also covered the achievements of successful men who reach the highest levels of wealth and innovation and proven that intellect and superior accomplishments come from a specific mindset and singleness of purpose. Also, intelligence is not measured by a degree or a test that's only good for a day. You can also do all that these men have done.

While many might believe that a college degree guarantees success, this is not always true. Likewise, not having one doesn't mean you've failed. However, these businessmen demonstrate that their lack of a degree did not stop them from becoming some of the most successful entrepreneurs in history.

Look at these individuals and their created accomplishments because they had a belief system with a work ethic. None have been based upon religion but faith in their purpose and goals, meaning is all "BELIEF."

Businesspeople Without Degrees

http://entreprenoria.com/personal-development/top-10-successful-entrepreneurs-without-a-college-degree/

1. Sir Richard Branson – Founder of Virgin Group

One of the world's best-known billionaires, Branson, was never a star in school. With a net worth estimated at $4.9 billion, the founder of Virgin Atlantic Airways, Virgin Records, Virgin Mobile, and other Virgin brands comprising over 400 companies never completed high school.

2. Dave Thomas — CEO of Wendy's

Thomas started working full-time at the Hobby House Restaurant in Fort Wayne, Indiana, while in high school before opening the first Wendy's outlet in 1969. Despite many ups and downs, the chain has always come out on top

3. Michael Dell — Founder of Dell Computers

Dell Computers founder Michael Dell attended The University of Texas for a short time before dropping out. As a college student, Michael built the foundations of what would ultimately become Dell Computers in his dorm room. His first few successes selling upgrades for personal computers led him to create a personal brand and grow his business considerably. The 27-year-old Dell became the youngest CEO on the Fortune 500 list in 1992. According to current estimates, he is worth $20 billion.

4. David Karp – Founder of Tumblr

David Karp, the founder of Tumblr, is another high school dropout who became a successful entrepreneur. After learning to code at 11 and obtaining an internship at 14, David Karp left high school to pursue his dream full-time. A blogging network that garnered 75,000 active followers within two weeks, he founded Tumblr with former co-worker Marco Arment in February 2007. Karp has a net worth of 200 million dollars and is 26 years old. His net worth grew to $1.1 billion following Yahoo! 's purchase of Tumblr in May of 2013.

5. John Mackey – Founder of Whole Foods

Though the founder of Whole Foods may have opted out of college, John Mackey wasn't a typical college student neither was he a slacker. Mackey enrolled as a student of philosophy and religion at the University of Texas before moving to San

Antonio and then finally dropping out of college. He launched the first Whole Foods Market in Austin. Mackey has a net worth of $100 million, despite donating his stock portfolio to charity and lowering his salary to a record $1 as of 2006.

6. Larry Ellison — founder of Oracle Systems

Former Oracle CEO Larry Ellison dropped out of two colleges before founding Software Development Laboratories (SDL) with two partners in 1977, after building databases for the CIA. Oracle Systems Corporation was the first company Ellison founded in 1982.

7. Anne Beiler, Auntie Anne's Pretzels

college and securing a degree were never crucial to Anne Beiler. In 1987, she set up a pretzel stand at a farmers' market in her locality to aid a $6000 loan she took from her in-laws. Anne's pretzels became so famous that she had recorded fantastic success with more than 100 franchise locations five years later.

8. Debbi Fields –Mrs. Fields Chocolate Chippery

In her junior year, fields dropped out of a community college to launch her company in 1977 from a loan she had secured from moneylenders. With no business experience, she started her first chocolate store named Mrs. Fields Chocolate Chipery in Palo Alto. The company had reached an impressive $400 million in revenue when she eventually decided to sell it in the 1990s.

9. Dov Charney –American Apparel

Dov Charney began selling clothes while still a high school student in Montreal. He was importing Fruit of the Loom and Hanes T-shirts from the United States and reselling them to fellow students and other Canadians. Initially selling his clothing wholesale, Charney opened his first retail outlets in 2003 in New York, Los Angeles, and Montreal. His company sold in 2006 for $360 million but stayed on as CEO.

10. Susan Lyne – CEO of AOL Brand Group

Despite having attended George Washington University, UC Berkeley, and an art school before leaving school, Susan Lyne's career in media shows that a college degree is not necessarily a yardstick for measuring success. Susan's rise started with her first primary job as an editor at Village Voice, before becoming the President and CEO of Martha Stewart Living Omnimedia, President of ABC Entertainment, and CEO of Gilt Group. She is a mother of four daughters as well as the chair of multiple boards. It is estimated that she is worth $ 4.7 million at present.

Matt Mullenweg

Despite dropping out of the University of Houston to work for CNET Networks, Matt Mullenweg founded WordPress, which powers 35% of the web today. In addition, it was he who founded Automattic, a company that serves household internet brands like WordPress, Akismet, Gravatar, and Tumblr. Currently, he manages the WordPress Foundation.

Mark Zuckerberg

Mark Zuckerberg built Facebook into the world's largest social network. During his sophomore year, Zuckerberg dropped out of Harvard in 2004 to work on Facebook full-time and remains its CEO to this day. Approximately $86.3 billion is now his net worth.

Pete Cashmore

Pete Cashmore founded the massively popular blog Mashable when he was just 19 years old without going to college. Despite not having a college degree, the Scottish businessman was able to sell Mashable to Ziff Davis for $50 million in 2017. The estimated net worth of Cashmore, who left the company in 2018, is approximately £90 million.

Daniel Ek

After just eight weeks of studying engineering at the Royal Institute of Technology in Sweden, Daniel Ek founded Spotify with his friends. As of today, the company has 217 million users worldwide.

Evan Williams

A year and a half after graduating from the University of Nebraska, Evan Williams pursued a career in information systems. As of 2016, his net worth is $2.2 billion. He co-founded Twitter in 2006 and published platforms Blogger and Medium later.

Bill Gates

Bill Gates, the billionaire co-founder of Microsoft, dropped out of Harvard to build his company. In a testament that degrees aren't always necessary, Bill Gates consistently ranked as the wealthiest man in the world from 1995 to 2017, when Amazon founder Jeff Bezos surpassed him.

Steve Jobs

A name synonymous with dropouts will always be Steve Jobs. In the case of Steve Jobs, Apple co-founder and creator of Pixar, it's no surprise how well that worked out for him.

Steve Wozniak,

Founded Apple and Steve Jobs (above) don't have a university degree to his credit. After being expelled from his first college, the University of Colorado Boulder, he dropped out of Berkeley for hacking the college's computer system. He now sits on an estimated net worth of $100 million.

Henry Ford

Henry Ford was born into extreme poverty. He went to school in a one-room class for eight years. Still, He learned his trade through apprenticeships, building the Ford Motor Company, revolutionizing manufacturing processes, and becoming one of history's richest men.

Walt Disney

Walt Disney (Centre), the founder of the Walt Disney Company, dropped out of high school at 16 to join the war effort, eventually gaining his first job as a commercial illustrator at the age of 18. He holds the record for most Academy Awards won by an individual with 22 from 59 nominations.

Benjamin Franklin

Despite that Benjamin Franklin only completed the second grade of his formal education, he was one of the most educated men of his day. Although he was not a doctor, he liked being called Doctor Franklin. As a result, Harvard and Yale conferred honorary degrees of Master of Arts upon him and honorary doctorates.

https://www.thegentlemansjournal.com/20-of-the-most-successful-businessmen-without-degrees/#:~:text=Richard%20Branson&text=The%20owner%20of%20Virgin%20dropped

Thomas Edison

Thomas Edison is credited with inventions such as the first practical incandescent light bulb and the phonograph. He held over 1,000 patents for his inventions.

Who Was Thomas Edison?

Thomas Edison was an American inventor who is considered one of America's leading businessmen and innovators. Edison rose from humble beginnings to work as an inventor of significant technology, including the first commercially viable incandescent light bulb with the help of Lewis Howard Latimer. The latter improved the process for the filaments for light bulbs. He is credited today for helping to build America's economy during the Industrial Revolution.

Early Life and Education

Edison was born on February 11, 1847, in Milan, Ohio. He was the youngest of seven children of Samuel and Nancy Edison. His father was an exiled political activist from Canada, while his mother was an accomplished school teacher and a significant influence in Edison's early life. An early bout with scarlet fever and ear infections left Edison with hearing difficulties in both ears as a child and nearly deaf as an adult.

Edison would later recount, with variations on the story, that he lost his hearing due to a train incident in which his ears were injured. But others have tended to discount this as the sole cause of his hearing loss.

In 1854, Edison's family moved to Port Huron, Michigan, where he attended public school for 12 weeks. A hyperactive child, prone to distraction, he was deemed "difficult" by his teacher.

His mother quickly pulled him from school and taught him at home. At age 11, he showed a voracious appetite for knowledge, reading books on many subjects. Edison developed a process for self-education and learning independently in this wide-open curriculum that would serve him throughout his life.

At age 12, Edison convinced his parents to sell newspapers to passengers along the Grand Trunk Railroad line. Exploiting his access to the news bulletins teletyped to the station office each day, Edison began publishing his small newspaper, called the Grand Trunk Herald.

The up-to-date articles were a hit with passengers. This was the first of what would become a long string of entrepreneurial ventures where he saw a need and capitalized on the opportunity.

Edison also used his access to the railroad to conduct chemical experiments in a small laboratory he set up in a train baggage car. Unfortunately, during one of his experiments, a chemical fire started, and the vehicle caught fire.

The conductor rushed in and struck Edison on the side of the head, probably furthering some of his hearing loss. He has kicked off the train and is forced to sell his newspapers at various stations along the route.

Edison the Telegrapher

While Edison worked for the railroad, a near-tragic event turned fortuitous for the young man. After Edison saved a three-year-old from being run over by an errant train, the child's grateful father rewarded him by teaching him to operate a telegraph. By age 15, he had learned enough to be employed as a telegraph operator.

For the next five years, Edison traveled throughout the Midwest as an itinerant telegrapher, subbing for those who had gone to the Civil War. He read widely, studied and experimented with telegraph technology, and became familiar with electrical science in his spare time.

In 1866, at age 19, Edison moved to Louisville, Kentucky, working for The Associated Press. The night shift allowed him to spend most of his time reading and experimenting. As a result, he developed an unrestricted style of thinking and inquiry, proving himself through objective examination and experimentation.

Initially, Edison excelled at his telegraph job because early Morse code was inscribed on a piece of paper, so Edison's partial deafness was no handicap. However, as the technology advanced, receivers were increasingly equipped with a sounding key, enabling telegraphers to "read" messages by the sound of the clicks. Unfortunately, this left Edison disadvantaged, with fewer and fewer opportunities for employment.

In 1868, Edison returned home to find his beloved mother was falling into mental illness and his father was out of work. The family was almost destitute. Edison realized he needed to take control of his future.

Upon the suggestion of a friend, he ventured to Boston, landing a job for the Western Union Company. At the time, Boston was America's center for science and culture, and Edison reveled in it. He designed and patented an electronic voting recorder for quickly tallying votes in the legislature in his spare time.

https://www.biography.com/inventor/thomas-edison

CHAPTER 14
TO CERTIFY OR NOT TO CERTIFY

I n a society that emphasis higher education and expressively imposes sanctions against the person without a college degree, what is so critically missed is that the dominant movers and shakers and employers of the significant corporations, most creators of innovations, are predominantly people with no college degree. These people represent some of the essential contributions without any higher education at all. A rule of thumb is if you don't have a degree, you better be successful in your business or invent an essential product to be counted and respected without a degree.

What does having a college degree mean? Is it higher education, or is it higher intelligence?

Or is it just a demonstration of a structured order?

Whereby self-education is the self-discipline to focus on a single trace for a single focus.

NOW LET US LOOK AT THE EVENTS OF THE WORLD IN BIBLICAL TIMES BC

- The Great Pyramids of Egypt 2630 BC

- Iron objects manufactured in ancient Near East 2500 BC

- Egyptians used papyrus and ink for writing 2500 BC

- Egyptians imported gold from other parts of Africa 2400 BC

- Sumerian King becomes first conqueror 2331 BC

- Horses domesticated in Egypt 2300 BC

- Ziggurats Built-in Mesopotamia 2100 BC

- Stonehenge was erected in England (estimated) 2000 BC

- Spoked wheels were invented in 1900 BC

- Hammurabi of Babylon provides the first written law code (estimated) 1750 BC

- Mexican Sun Pyramid built 1500 BC

- First metalworking in South America 1440 BC

- Water Clock invented in Egypt 1400 BC

- The Palace of Knossos on the island of Crete was destroyed by an earthquake in 1380 BC

- King Tutankhamen was buried in Egypt amidst great treasure 1358 BC

- Silk fabrics manufactured 1250 BC

- First Chinese dictionary 1200 BC

- Destruction of Troy during Trojan War 1183 BC

- Mayans settled in the Yucatan peninsula 1000 BC

- Native Americans in California build wood-reed houses 1000 BC

- Gold vessels and jewelry popular in Northern Europe 950 BC

- Celts invade Britain 900 BC

- Evidence of highly developed metal and stone sculptures in Africa 850 BC

- Founding of Carthage 814 BC

- Homer's Thad and Odyssey written down 800 BC

- First, known Olympics occurs 776 BC

- Legendary date for the founding of Rome 753 BC

- Earliest musical notation in Greece 750 BC

- Shedu Assyrian statue made of limestone "8th century BC."

- First known lock and key in the palace in Assyria 710 BC

- False teeth were invented in Italy 700 BC

- Japan was founded as a nation 660 BC

- Soldering of irons originated 650 BC

- Horse Racing held at the 33rd Olympics 648 BC

- Nineveh was destroyed 612 BC

- The Temple of Artemis was constructed in Ephesus 600 BC

- Greek astronomer Thales predicts eclipse 585 BC

- Pythagoras, a Greek philosopher and mathematician, is born 582 BC

- Gautama Buddha, the founder of Buddhism, is born in India in 563 BC

- Aesop writes his fables 560 BC

- Confucious is born 551 BC

- Cyrus the Great conquers the Medes founding the Persian Empire 550 BC

- Horseback postal service in the Persian Empire 540 BC

- Cyrus of Persia overthrew Babylon 539 BC

- Polo was played as a sport in Persia 525 BC

- Public libraries open in Athens, Greece 520 BC

- Rome became a republic in 509 BC

- Greeks repel Persia in the battle of Marathon 490 BC

- Socrates, a famous philosopher, is born 469 BC

- Hippocrates, the father of modern medicine, is born 460 BC

- The Golden Age in Athens Greece 457 BC

- The Parthenon was built in Athens, Greece, 448 BC

- Plato, a famous philosopher, is born 429 BC

- Socrates was condemned to death 399 BC

- Aristotle is born 384 BC

- Plato writes the Republic 370 BC

- Alexander the Great defeats the Persian Empire 330 BC

- Romans build the first paved road, the Appian Way 312 BC

- Roman conquers Sicily 241 BC

- Great Walls of China-made 215 BC

- Antiochus IV plunders Jerusalem Temple 169 BC

- Judas Maccabeus begins a revolt against Antiochus IV 165 BC

- Jews and astrologers were banished from Rome 139 BC

- First Chinese ships reach the coast of India 102 BC

- Julius Caesar first emperor of Rome is born 100 BC

- Romans conquered England 55 BC

- Cleopatra becomes the last independent Egyptian ruler 51 BC

- Julius Caesar becomes dictator for life, assassinated two years later 46 BC

- Romans make Herod the Great King of Judea 37 BC

- Cleopatra and Marc Anthony commit suicide 30 BC

- Sumo wrestling in Japan 23 BC

- Herod the Great begins remodeling Temple in Jerusalem 20 BC

THE EVENTS
OF THE WORLD IN BIBLICAL TIMES AD

- Saddles were first used in Europe AD 1

- Judea becomes a Roman province AD 6

- Zealots in Judea rebel against Rome AD 7

- Tiberius succeeds Caesar Augustus as Roman emperor AD 14

- Caligula becomes the Roman emperor AD 37

- Herod Agrippa was appointed king of Judea AD 40

- Claudius becomes the Roman emperor AD 41

- Romans begin using soap AD 50

- Emperor Claudius was poisoned by order of his wife AD 54

- Nero Becomes the Roman emperor AD 54

- Fire burns Rome, Nero blames Christians AD 64

- Paintings on canvas AD 66

- Romans destroy a religious commune at Qumran AD 68

- China opens silk trade with the West AD 74

- Romans begin construction on the Colosseum AD 75

- Mount Vesuvius erupts AD 79

- Domitian becomes the Roman emperor AD 81

TIMES OF JESUS CHRIST

- Jesus Christ is Born 6 BC

- Herod the Great dies 4 AD

- Paul is born around 5 AD

- Jesus arrives at the Temple as a boy 6 AD

- Jesus Christ BC 6-AD 30

- Matthew, BC 6-AD 30

- Luke, BC 6-AD 30

- Mark, AD 26-30 AD

- John, AD 26-30 AD

- John the Baptist begins his ministry AD 26

- Jesus begins his ministry AD 27

- John the Baptist is beheaded AD 29

- Jesus is executed by crucifixion AD 30

- The Holy Spirit descends on the Day of Pentecost AD 30

THE CHURCH BEGINS.

- AD 30-Present

- Saul's conversion on the Damascus Road AD 35

- Acts AD 30 -60

- The transformation of Cornelius AD 40

- Paul begins his first missionary journey AD 46

- James, AD 48

- The Jerusalem Council AD 49

- Galatians, AD 49

- 1 & 2 Thes. AD 50

- Paul begins his third missionary journey AD 51

- 1 Corinth, AD 53

- 2 Corinth, Romans, AD 54

- Paul in prison in Caesarea AD 57

- Paul's voyage to Rome AD 59

- Col, Phlm, & Eph, AD 60

- Phil, AD 61

- 1 Tim & Titus, AD 62

- Paul was released from prison in Rome AD 62

- Paul Martyred AD 64

- 2Tim & 1 Peter, AD 64

- 2 Peter, AD 65

- Hebrews & Jude, around AD 66

- Rome destroys Jerusalem AD 70

- Jews commit mass suicide at Masada AD 73

- 1 John, between AD 80-90

- 2 & 3 John around AD 90

- Revelation, AD 95

"These timelines provided by the Chronological Life Application Study Bible."

As you realized, critical events of the past, considering their roles and the impact they have made, we can place ourselves in timelines that cannot be refuted by the importance they have on our lives.

THREE-PART MIND

The psychoanalyst and theorist Sigmund Freud (1856-1939) is widely recognized as the father of psychoanalysis.

We are shaped by the events of our childhood, according to Freud. Traumatic experiences in one's past can cause anxiety hidden from consciousness, eventually causing problems in adulthood (in the form of neuroses).

When we describe our behavior to ourselves or others (conscious mental activity), we rarely accurately account for our motivations, not because we deliberately lie. Humans are adept at deceiving others, but they are even better at deceiving themselves.

The goal of Freud's life was to find ways of penetrating this often subtle and elaborate camouflage that obscures the hidden structures and processes of the psyche.

He became part of the vocabulary of Western society through his lexicon. People today use words he introduced through his theories, such as anal-retentive personality, libido, denial, repression, cathartic, Freudian slip, and neurotic.

Freud (1915) found that some events and desires were often too painful or frightening for his patients. But, unfortunately, many believed such information was buried in the unconscious mind as a result of repression.

Sigmund Freud stressed the importance of the unconscious mind. One of the central assumptions of Freudian psychology is that the unconscious mind governs behavior to a greater extent than most people believe. Thus, the purpose of psychoanalysis is to bring the unconscious to consciousness.

The Psyche model Freud developed later (1923) comprises id, ego, and superego (after this referred to by Freud as "the psychic apparatus"). It is not a physical part of the brain but rather a conceptualization of essential mental functions. Most conceptualized as three are the id, ego, and superego, which have crucial aspects of the human personality.

According to the pleasure principle, Freud assumed the id operated at an unconscious level (gratification from satisfying basic instincts). Thus, the id comprises two kinds of biological instincts (or drives) which Freud called Eros and Thanatos.

Eros, or life instinct, helps the individual survive; it directs life-sustaining activities such as respiration, eating, and sex (Freud, 1925). The energy created by the life instincts is known as libido.

In contrast, Thanatos, or death instinct, is viewed as a set of destructive forces present in all human beings (Freud, 1920). When this energy is directed outward onto others, its expressed as aggression and violence. Freud believed that Eros is stronger than Thanatos, thus enabling people to survive rather than self-destruct.

The ego develops from the id during infancy. The ego's goal is to satisfy the id's demands in a safe and socially acceptable way. In contrast to the id, the ego follows the reality principle as it operates in both the conscious and the unconscious mind.

Sigmund Freud's Theories - Simply Psychology.
https://www.simplypsychology.org/Sigmund-Freud.html

The superego develops during early childhood (when the child identifies with the same-sex parent) and ensures moral standards. The superego operates on the morality principle and motivates us to behave socially responsible and acceptable. The fundamental dilemma of all human existence is that each element of the psychic apparatus makes demands upon us incompatible with the other two. Inner conflict is inevitable.

Using the example of the superego can make us feel guilty about not following rules.

An ego must mediate a conflict between the superego and its id to resolve it. The ego can deploy various defense mechanisms to prevent itself from becoming overwhelmed by anxiety (Freud, 1894, 1896).

Sigmund Freud's Theories - Simply Psychology.
https://www.simplypsychology.org/Sigmund-Freud.html

CHAPTER 15

WHAT DO YOU BELIEVE?

Self-talk is critically essential, and so are affirmations; both are declarations to your Spirit of higher intelligence, in my case, the God I serve. When we self-talk, we are spinning time with our spirit. With affirmations, we are giving a call to action to the Spirit to perform, but you must first understand affirmations and have the right to use them. Only your spirit can help you to understand. God tells us to trust in him. Again, I say, "Trust in God," act on faith. Stir up the gift that is within you. God's gift to man is the Holy Spirit. Afterward, you should receive power which the Holy Spirit comes on you. Today this Spirit and its Power are denied because of a lack of knowledge.

Today the body of Christ lacks the backbone to say what God has told them to say, the whole truth. It is clear where the body of Christ has its shortcoming. They have a form of Godliness, but they deny the power thereof. You cannot go where the mind won't take you, and how can they hear without a teacher? That teacher must first truly understand and receive God's message to tell you the news. Hence, the reason the (Holy Spirit) Comforter is so grieved; he is stuck with flesh to contend with God's word.

It does not communicate with flesh, only the spirit. Jesus states you must be born again. Before Jesus, God spoke to prophets, and after Jesus, the Holy Spirit speaks to man. He said, therefore I must go away, or else you cannot receive me. Jesus came to re-establish communication between man and God. He did so at the cross and completed it when the stone rolled away, and he walked out of the tomb. The day Adam sinned, he lost the image of God; the day you repented, accepted Christ, and were born again, you became the image of God.

If Jesus wasn't the point of beginning, why did God send Jesus? He had already created a perfect man in his image; it is a serious question that God created a man who didn't obey him and had imperfections, created an Angel, and he had contention against him and wanted to be like God. Everything God created was by his design, so why would he purposely put in a flaw in his creation? Why would he even want to be content with all these errors in the human race and watch as generations pass, killing off one another? Exactly what have we missed here?

He sends Moses up to the mountain top to receive the ten commandments; after all the miracles the believers had seen, they created a golden calf to worship in Moses's absence. Then God puts the laws on a stone table, specifically stating thou shall not kill. But, might I add, no one has been able to find it? The three most essential pieces missing are the ten commandments God created, the Ark of the Covenant, which no unclean person could even come near because it would destroy anyone who did. And it was taken by an unruly king against God's power.

God designed the Ark of The Covenant and is missing off the face of the Earth. These, at the very least, would have been protected and preserved. Then Noah in his family was the transition of the new beginning. Noah's family was the fresh start of man, but where did all the other races of people appear? None of this deters me from my belief in God or Jesus, but it indeed tells the story of man. We know Jesus came, and he performed everything that the witnesses wrote. I do not doubt God as creator; I have problems with some of his creations. Jesus's coming is no coincidence; it was about making a new covenant with man to bring us back into the kingdom, which he accomplished through the Comforter.

Through reconciliation, the Comforter, and God's covenant with the high priest, you are sealed in the perfection of his image by the "Supernatural" when you are "Born Again." God does not need you to understand how you must be born again. He states that you must be; it perfects God's plan with him. He received us back unto himself. Understanding the fusion of God and Man is so critically important. Your only requirement now is that you believe. That's always Jesus's question, "Do you believe?" As John baptized Jesus, he received the Holy Spirit and immediately began his ministry.

He shows us its power through his miracles; these are examples of what we are supposed to do after the Holy Spirit comes upon us. Christians do not want to understand this because many do not believe they have the "Mind of Christ." (1 Corinthians 2:16). After all, we have the Comforter. We are sealed until he redeems us because of the Holy Spirit, and that all begins with the High Priest Jesus. He had to wait to start his ministry under the customs at that time, which was the High priest had been at least 30 years of age.

The high priest was the only one during this time that could make the offering for the believers. He would present an offering to God to have his offering accepted or rejected at the Holy of Holies. The Ark of the Covenant was located in a portable shrine known as the tabernacle. They would hang a curtain to prevent people from seeing it because it was holy. According to prophecy, the messiah had to come through the bloodline of David, and he was also 30 when he came into power.

When the high priest presents offerings, the offerings are either accepted or rejected by God. If the offerings are received, the blessings of the High Priest would be on all the people covered under the high priest as long as he is alive and would also cease when he dies. It did not matter what these people had done or where they came from; as long as they were under the high priest, the blessing remained until he died. If his offering was accepted, it stayed with the high priest. Among them could have been thieves, murderers, rapists, and prostitutes. The blessing was with the high priest, and that was God's covenant.

But if the high priest offering was refused, he and his followers did not receive the blessing of God over him or his people. It didn't matter if they were the most beautiful people on the planet, doctors, lawyers, teachers, carpenters, or others; they were not covered. The sealing happened with Jesus; he is the high priest that will never die; so whenever a person comes to him, they are blessed and sealed until the day of redemption because he was the perfect offering without blemishes.

God sent his Son to free the captive from carnality and realign the creation in proper alignment with himself; by doing so, he had to have an unblemished sacrifice holy and acceptable. It had to be a high priest that would be everlasting since the Comforter cannot cease to exist. God knew beforehand that he would be sending the Comforter. God cannot cease to exist; it would be a conflict of sovereign nature; he is immortal. It is where believing and being born again is pivotal and trusting in God is critical because at this very point is where we are sealed.

This is why he says, "lean not to your understanding," and he also states that his mind is much higher than the mind of the man, and he is telling you, you cannot compare. He said to Thomas if he could believe without seeing him and touching his wounds, how much better it would have been. He was bruised for our iniquities. This is why he said Father forgive them, for they know not what they do. So when a person comes to Jesus and is born again, the sealing takes place regardless because of the covenant of the high priest.

We pass from death unto life when we received salvation because Jesus the high priest was found blameless and eternal, and our sins are covered under Jesus as high priest. We will not see death; if God lives inside of you, why would he judge himself? A house divided against itself cannot stand. So why would I be saved, sealed, and then judged?

CHINESE BAMBOO STORY

With a seed so hard it won't grow for almost five years when planted in the ground, the Chinese bamboo tree is a testament to one's faith. First and second years, third and fourth years, do not bring anything to fruition. Despite your efforts, you will not see the result of your labor for all those years. That is, until the fifth year.

During the fifth year, the seed breaks through the soil and begins to grow into a tree. It grows. The Chinese bamboo tree has raised upwards of 3 feet a day, almost 90 feet in about a

191

month. You can stand there and watch it shoot up! (It has been timed at approximately one inch of growth every 40 minutes.)

Now, if the person who planted the seed had failed to water it or maintain the ground during those five years, the kernel would have died. The kernel would have died if the planter had gotten tired of waiting and dug up the seed to find out what was taking so long or walked away in disgust. The lesson here is true faith in what you believe requires patience and persistence.
http://www.bobgarneronline.com/blog/personal-development/chinese-bamboo-tree-the-3-hidden-messages/

STORY OF THE AFRICAN DIAMOND HUNTER

There was a man who had a large piece of land in Africa. It sat alongside the river where he would sit every day fishing and hoping he could one day find himself diamonds as he had heard. So, he decided to do something about it and go on a journey to become rich. So, he sold his land and decided to do just that. He owned hundreds of acres of land adjacent to the water, and it was very rough and rocky. Surely someone would buy his property. And yes, they did; he was off and running.

He travels all over Africa, looking to strike it rich, looking for his diamonds. He searched until he ran out of money; years had gone by, so he began traveling back toward the land he had sold. When he arrived back, he noticed the landscape had changed. There was a massive number of machines sitting around and buildings built on the property. He approached the new owner and asked what had happened. After you sold me the land, he said, I went fishing alongside the river, where I first contacted you to buy the property.

That day you were fishing, and I noticed how nice the spot you were sitting felt and how beautiful it looked. So, the first day after we closed, I went fishing. I enjoyed it so much for three weeks. Then, I fished the same spot, and one day I noticed a glittering place in the water, a ray of a beam, a dazzling light. So, I got in the water to inspect, and it was a big rough rock with shiny spots, so I took it to a person that knows about these things.

Come to find out; it was a diamond. It was not just a diamond, but the biggest one found to date in all of Africa. And they were all over the place.

The moral of the story is he was sitting on acres of diamonds, but he failed to do his research on his land before he went out to search for a diamond elsewhere. He had vast amounts of riches, but he was in a hurry and didn't look. He later committed suicide.

If he had taken the time to do exhaustive research on the assets he had in his possession, investigate his toolbox. Most of us have things of value but lack the understanding of how to make them work. Failure to measure the value of time is the most expensive mistake you can make.

One of the greatest life lessons I have ever learned is owning it for life when I sow a seed. The seed may leave my hands or my mouth, but I will hold the harvest of that seed for life. So, it does not matter what you sow; you will reap the kind of that seed.

STOP FIGHTING CHANGE AND LIVE BY FAITH

Stop fighting change. It's futile to try and bend a river. We can only use the force and adapt to its positive energy or let it be a wrecking ball. If you persist in such foolishness, you will have better success at emptying an Olympic size pool with a teaspoon than preventing life's path of change.

This same force of change happens when the tools available to you are used and understood; you open doors no man can shut. The power of your faith is the evidence of things not seen. Religion and belief are not the same; Faith will materialize when you see it in completion. Faith is the end of the beginning of your imagination or the image you see.

https://www.simplypsychology.org/simplypsychology.org-Sigmund-Freud.pdf

THE SOONER YOU RELEASE YOUR SEED
THE SOONER THE HARVEST

When we think of seeds, we think of a garden or a farm with plant sapling or maybe just a seed. They are tangible or metaphors; regardless of the properties of your plant, they can have the same impact as a gain or a loss. Whatsoever a man sows, he will reap. When you plant a seed into the soil, it does not care what you sowed; it only receives what you planted. In contrast, it is faithful in its responsibility to return the harvest to the Sower. Many have read from the bible; we reap what we sow.

Galatians 6:7-9

King James Version

7 Be not deceived; God is not mocked: for whatsoever a man soweth, that shall he also reap.

8 For he that soweth to his flesh shall of the flesh reap corruption, but he that soweth to the Spirit shall of the Spirit reap life everlasting.

9 And let us not be weary in well doing: for in due season, we shall reap if we faint not.

The laws of success do not care; instead, you are religious or not; every great success happens because a person believes it and sticks with it, end of the story.

Joshua 1:8

King James Version

8 This book of the law shall not depart out of thy mouth, but thou shalt meditate therein day and night, that thou mayest observe to do according to all that is written therein: for then thou shalt make thy way prosperous, and then thou shalt have good success.

"Every day Joshua meditated on what was written; what was written was now his goals and commitment."

If you were to look at the people around you in the world, like Bill Gates and Melinda Gates, whom we all know as the Founders of Microsoft with titles as the world's wealthiest people, you would think they had no problems. Unfortunately, that can be nothing further from the truth. They deal with systemic humanism—lust, adultery, greed, and lack of self-control.

They made all the money one can dream of in a perfect world, legally and gracious. However, they maintain their wealth because they violate their oaths and rights and not the rights of others. To be clear, the two became one in marriage, so they injured themselves.

Warren Buffet made his wealth through investing in the art of patience, like the story of the Chinese Bamboo Tree. He understands time and value and is in love with the idea that the proverb of patience is a virtue. He has maintained his wealth throughout generations and always recovers through time. Although he is not financially intelligent, he understood the value of simplicity.

The Billionaire with the Trillion-dollar company, Elon Musk is a chameleon lizard character; he is a product of timing and understands that resources in people are not measured by degrees but by visionary intelligence. He understands the image-maker is the evolutionary architect of the futuristic advancements, which are hidden realities seeking to loosen. He wants the world to think he is a genius and mysterious; he is not. He thinks he is. He reaches a level of success that even surprised him, and after he has seen the weakness and how easy it was to manipulate people through tweets, he played with their life, which affected the world as the Joker and puppet maker. **This chapter is not closed yet!!!!**

When seeds fall into the unfertilized ground and never take root, the result is Jeffrey Epstein. He was a financier and socialite who made hundreds of millions only to lose his wealth, freedom, and later, he lost his life. As a professor at a private school, most would say he was brilliant. Usually, we think more of ourselves than we ought and find out later we are alone, traveling 100 miles per hour on the road with a bridge to nowhere. Success is given to all who are willing to work for it. How we live our lives is essential, more than what we allow to control us through selfish actions of moral failures in lust, only to be put to shame and utterly publicly disgraced.

Finally, former President Donald J. Trump and Billionaire, to most, he is the Guru of deal-making, to others the all-time biggest fraudster. To some, he is the greatest. Some say the president of the big deception. In my opinion, he is Donald J.

Trump. Fact-checking had him clocked as the biggest liar on the planet, but the truth is he understands the mind of man better than anybody I have ever met. He was taught at Church by the best teachers who understood how the mind works with human emotion, giving him the edge on any unsuspecting person. His teacher may have understood the fusion of proper engagement with Christ and man through the Holy Spirit. That association was by one of America's most famous ministers, the Rev. Norman Vincent Peale.

Donald J. Trump knows how truth is established, and he creates and develops whatever truth he wants and needs. After realizing his power, it reminds me of Elon Musk, toying around with the world as if it belongs to him and him alone; the two are similar in many ways, with some exceptions, meaning Elon. So, he does not lie, he makes millions of people believe it, and it is true to him who wants to believe. The subconscious mind only responds by completing, satisfying, and fulfilling your desire when accepted by the subconscious mind.

He always had an ace in the hole before and afterward; that is why he picked Elisabeth Dee DeVos as United States Secretary of Education. He knew one day he would more than likely need a military and guerrilla warfare strategist — a private security company with the highest-level clearance and access. He knows her association and relationship intimately, which may be why the republican party all follow his suit on any and every action, good or bad, out of fear.

Seed returns to the Sower without prejudice.

DNA DOWNLOAD

Case of self-worth

Many have no idea of their great value or self-worth. Well, if you understood what great opportunities await you, you could live in total freedom. Still, we allow situations to change our lives without the facts; following conspiracy theories and political parties and religious leaders sold out to these parties instead of the faith they boast is precious. Most do not know what powers they have if they only knew how to live in their belief system if they only believe. You are born with everything you need. You, understanding how to use Mind, Body, and Spirit, demystify your life's purpose. This inventory list puts you on equal footing as any person alive, and they have nothing more.

Inventory list:

- Time 24 hours
- Seven days
- Two hands (Majority)
- Two arms (Majority)
- Two legs (Majority)
- Two feet (Majority)
- Two eyes (Majority)
- One mouth
- One nose
- One brain

- Two ears (Majority)
- Ten fingers (Majority)
- Ten toes (Majority)
- Private parts
- Develop/undeveloped mine.
- Skillset
- Toolbox
- Mindset
- One of Six Billion sperm cells
- (Race intentionally left out)
- One core belief system (optional)
- Singleness of Purpose (optional)
- DNA Package installed
- Environmental viruses (Acquired over time) Goals package (optional) Culture mode off.

Your Mind:

Single-use purpose is conscious

***Completely DNA download ***

100 percent owned by host

***100 percent subconscious support ***

Time expires upon use, cannot be replaced

*** Time has unlimited resources and potential.

***Time is priceless ***

*** Time does not discriminate ***

Natural resources:
Gold, Silver, Platinum, and Diamonds.

Fluctuations in values*

***Is limited in supply ***

***Replaceable ***

Limited to individual buyers

***Most of us have 100% of the above inventory list. Still, our mental tools have remained obstructed by alternative thinking, limited understanding, and lack of knowledge of engaging this life we live. ***

CHAPTER 16

PHYSICAL FIVE SENSES:[NATURAL HARDWARE]

U NDERSTANDING THE SENSORY ORGANS AND THEIR FUNCTIONS: Detecting stimuli is the job of sensory organs. Neurons carry nerve impulses from receptors to the brain (sensory nerves carry nerve impulses from receptors). Nerve signals are received by the brain, interpreted, and then acted upon. The brain sends nerve impulses through the nerves (motor nerves, which send signals from the CN to muscles, glands, etc.). The effectors of the body are the parts that perform responses (muscles, glands).

STEP BY STEP - STIMULUS TO REACTION:

Detecting and responding to stimuli is the function of the nervous system. When an organism is stimulated, it reacts. We call this reaction a response. There are receptors in every sensory organ that are highly responsive to stimulants. Stimulation of sensory receptors in the organ leads to nerve impulses. Nerves generate electric impulses. Nerve impulses travel along nerves (sensory nerves transmit nerve signals from receptors to the brain). Nerve signals are received by the brain, interpreted, and then acted upon. Then the brain sends nerve impulses through the nerves (motor nerves, transmitting nerve impulses from the central nervous system to muscles or glands) to the effectors. An effector is a part of the body that carries out a response (muscles, glands).

FACULTIES OF THE MIND (SOFTWARE)
FACULTIES:

The faculties are the tools of the brain, not to be confused with the senses. The faculties are the tools embedded in the mind managed by the Ego and fear. The Ego only wants control and power even with internal force, which is disruptive and self-destructive. It does not care about anything except defending its position of power.

Six Faculties:

Imagination: The faculty or action of forming new ideas, images, or concepts of external objects not present to the senses.

The imagination is probably one of the greatest miracles of human beings. It is through the images that we have enjoyed many advancements beyond belief. Our beautiful ability to invent things that have transformed our lives came from this. By understanding how these higher faculties work, we can utilize them to achieve anything we desire in life. Our Creator has given us the tools. However, we need to build them to a higher level.

Imagination, or Visualization, may be defined as the formation of mental images or pictures. A person forms a thought, an idea in their mind, that corresponds to or matches the thought or idea. For example, suppose a person thinks of a boat. In that case, they don't particularly feel the word "boat" – they almost invariably form an image of a ship they have encountered at some previous moment in time—a boat seen only as a picture in a book.

Napoleon Hill Think and Grow Rich:

There are no limitations to the mind except those we acknowledge

Reasoning: The act of thinking about something in a logical, sensible way.

Our reasoning factor enables us to think and desire anything. Each of these faculties can be used to think and act in a human being. In contrast, an animal acts based on instinct. By reason, we mean to form conclusions, judgments, or inferences based on facts or premises. A specific point or belief is selected and used to establish a conclusion, conclusion review, or conclusion deduction. People will choose their facts or hypotheses from either of two areas: Ideas they have formulated and reside in their objective or conscious mind and information conveyed to the objective or conscious mind via the physical senses.

Isaiah 1:18-2:11

New King James Version

18 "Come now, and let us reason together," Says the Lord, "Though your sins are like scarlet,

They shall be as white as snow; Though they are red like crimson, they shall be as wool.

19 If you are willing and obedient, you shall eat the good of the land; 20 But if you refuse and rebel,

The sword shall devour you; For the mouth of the Lord has spoken.

Intuition is an ability, or characteristic one possesses that is derived from instinct rather than conscious thought.

A person's intuition is the state of becoming aware of some condition and recognizing it without actively engaging their senses. Thus, intuition is indeed a mental process. However, intuition can be defined as an instantaneous idea or response we receive without even thinking about it. In other words, intuition can be explained as the ability to perceive truth, fact, etc., independently of reason.

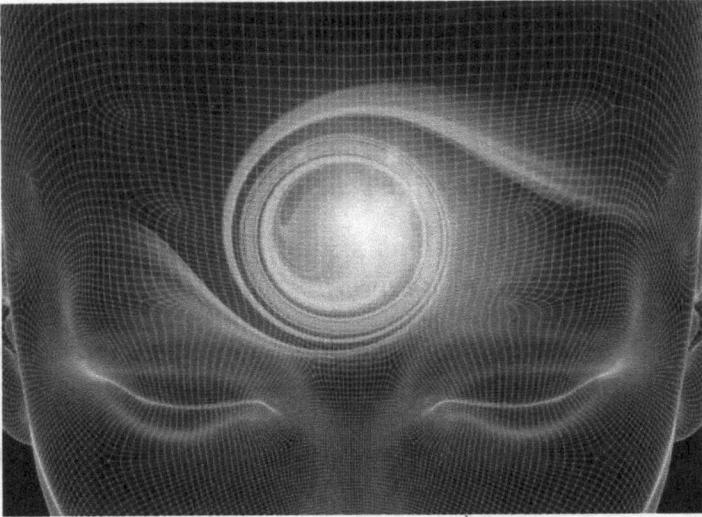

Memory: Memory refers to the processes that enable information to be acquired, stored, retained, and later retrieved. Memory involves three significant functions: encoding, storage, and retrieval — our ability to remember the information we have acquired or experienced consists of preserving knowledge and retrieving it.

Some people claim they have terrible memories; I strongly doubt this is true. It is possible to memorize anything. However, considering the claims of Jim Rohn, we may lack an adequate memory and therefore need to build up our mental muscles by utilizing and validating one of the faculties. 'Memory' is defined as the ability to retain, recall or recognize past events, emotions, impressions, etc. A general summary of facts, circumstances, beliefs, experiences, etc., can be achieved by referring to information.

Perception: The process of seeing, hearing, or detecting something through one's senses to comprehend, comprehend, or understand something; the mental representation of something.

PERCEPTION IS A TOOL
THAT'S POINTED
ON BOTH ENDS.

HANNIBAL'

There can be two different perspectives on the same object when two people look at it. Their perception of things is different. It is impossible to say right or wrong in this instance. It is just a difference of opinion. The dictionary describes perception as the act or faculty of recognizing something using the senses or the mind. Hence, we form an opinion about a subject or object by developing ideas about it out of what we perceive with our senses (sight, hearing, smell, taste, and touch).

The Will:
Humans possess the capacity and freedom to choose between alternatives or take action in particular circumstances regardless of natural, social, or divine restraints. Thus, the principle of freedom of choice is a critical element of existentialism. All humanity, unregenerate and regenerate throughout the Bible, possess inherent freedom of choice if we understand "free will" as an unrestrained, voluntary act.

Only the mind which sets it in motion can maintain its ability to focus solely on an idea and to ignore everything else. Mental faculties such as will, when used correctly, are used to keep an image in the mind. You might be surprised to discover that "Wills" are easier than they sound once you know what they are and what they are not.

CHAPTER 17

MALWARE & VIRUSES
OF THE MIND

Gossip is the worst thing you can ever do; by all means, avoid the conversation and the people who bring it. These are very toxic people looking for drama and to stir up bad situations and, in most cases, make things even worse. They are the ones transferring corrupt files into your mental vault and corrupting vibrations into the atmosphere leading to a toxic environment. When this seed has remained planted, it reaps the same as weeds in a garden. The author of the minefield of mental debris, all corrupt files are laden with malware and viruses. They reside here in the negative emotions uploaded by people in your circle of friends and family you trust.

Instead of invited or uninvited, the gate to your mind must be kept high and closed at all entries. Captivity of words remains the norm in any circumstances, never let your guard down in this area or get comfortable; it is a slippery slope to disaster. Just master the art of reset and never stay in a begrudging situation. If it's someone close to you, love them from a distance but forgive them for any misunderstanding and mistake that offended you.

Forgiveness is your weapon of power. Though some may see it as a sign of weakness, forgiveness is a weapon of strength in your arsenal of mental weapons. It keeps you free and debugged of pestilence situations. Finally, you are managing what gets a free ride in your head. Forgiveness is not for them; every time you forgive, you delete mental debris, and you can wipe it completely when you show love afterward….at a distance, of course. Showing love gives it no chance to go to the recycle bin. When you master forgiveness and input, every day is a clean sheet of paper with unlimited possibilities of hope.

These drivers trigger impulse reactions to events without warning, and all are associated with the drifter's mentality. We are either drifters or non-drifter. If you go with the flow, you are a drifter, and if you manage life's events by the day, you are a non-drifter. Most drifters you will find at the pawnshop and title loans because they are ill-prepared to handle life's situations that arrive without warnings. Let's look at the meaning of each fear. Napoleon Hill, Think and Grow Rich, understood the natural and basic spiritual knowledge of the truth but lacked knowledge of spirit fusion.

"Think And Grow Rich is considered the most excellent book on success of all time."

Among the best books on success in history, Think and Grow Rich is considered the best. Napoleon Hill devoted approximately 25 years of his life studying the most successful individuals, finding out the key aspect that made them successful, and making the other 98% of the world mediocre or average. With this understanding of his work of successful people, we must also acknowledge that they were human. Mr. Hill also had a unique sense of spiritual matters, just as other ministers then and now lack the proper understanding and interpretation of the truth of the fusion of man and Spirit.

211

To acknowledge the proper understanding would mean most would have to admit their failure of spiritual knowledge or flat-out frauds. Believers today are weakened by the loss of this outright omission that denies the believer the full power of the Holy Spirit. A person that repents does have a place in eternity, then fails to comprehend the use of the power is the poor in spirit, even though theirs is the kingdom of God. He that comes unto me I will, at no wise cast out, and they are sealed until the day of redemption.

This is only because of the promises, the covenant, and that God does not change. So, in the one interpretation, man's empowerment and enlightenment switch on. He concluded that when trying to figure out what makes people fail to reach their goals, there are 30 significant causes. It is very substantial that Napoleon Hill pointed these causes out because if you aren't yet successful, you can go down the list and figure out which of the reasons apply to you, so you are aware of them and can address them.

SIX FEARS THAT PLAGUE OUR LIVES:
FEAR OF POVERTY

Fear of Poverty: Napoleon Hill in Think and Grow Rich Discusses the Destructive Power of The Fear of Poverty

1. The Six Ghosts of FEAR and How to Be victorious.

2. How to Outwit the Six Ghosts of Fear

   - BEFORE You Can Put Any Portion of This Philosophy into Successful Use, the mind Must Be Ready to Receive It.

   - The Preparation Is Not Difficult.

3. **It Begins with a Study, Analysis, And Understanding of Three Enemies You Must Clear Out of INDECISION, DOUBT, and FEAR**

   • The faculties will be dysfunctional while these three negatives or any of them remain in your mind.

   • The members of this unholy trio are closely related; where one is found, the other two are close at hand.

4. **INDECISION is the seedling of FEAR!**

   • Indecision crystallizes into DOUBT, the two blend, and become FEAR!

   • The "blending" process often is slow.

   • This is one reason why these three enemies are so dangerous.

   • They germinate and grow without their presence observed.

5. **INDECISION, DOUBT, and FEAR**

   • They must be understood by all who accumulate riches, whether measured in terms of money or a state of mind of far greater value than money.

   • Do not be deceived by the habits of these subtle enemies.

   • Sometimes, they remain hidden in the subconscious mind, difficult to locate, and still more challenging to eliminate.

6. **HUMANITY Is Plagued by SIX BASIC FEARS!**

   • There are six basic fears, with some combination of which every human suffers at one tune or another.

- Most people are fortunate if they do not suffer from the entire six.

7. **Listed in order of most common occurrence are six basic fears**

    1. Poverty

    2. Criticism

    3. Ill Health

    4. Loss of Love of Someone

    5. Old Age

    6. Death

8. **FEARS Are Nothing More Than States of Your Mind That You Can Control by Changing Your Thoughts!**

    - All other fears are of minor importance.

    - They can be grouped under these six headings.

    - The prevalence of these fears, as a curse to the world, runs in cycles.

    - For almost six years, while the depression was on, we floundered in the cycle of FEAR OF POVERTY.

9. **Individual FEARS Adversely Affect Human History in a Big Way!**

    - During the world war, we were in the cycle of FEAR OF DEATH.

    - Just following the war, we were in the cycle of FEAR OF ILL HEALTH, as evidenced by the 1918 Spanish Influenza Pandemic of disease that spread itself all over the world, killing millions.

214

- Fears are nothing more than states of mind.

10. You Are in Total Control of Your Minds by Choosing Your Thoughts!

- Your state of mind is subject to control and direction.
- Physicians, as everyone knows, are less subject to attack by disease than ordinary laypeople because they DO NOT FEAR DISEASE.

11. FEAR Of Sickness Creates the Disease You Fear!

- Physicians, without fear or hesitation, have treated large numbers of patients with contagious diseases such as smallpox without becoming infected.
- Their immunity against the disease consisted mainly of their absolute lack of FEAR, if not solely.
- Humans can create nothing that does not first exist in the form of an impulse of thought.

12. Our thoughts are equivalent to our internal impulses.

13. Every Human Being Has the Ability to Completely Control Their Mind

- You can open your mind to the negative thought impulses released by other brains or close the doors tightly and admit only thought impulses you choose.
- You have absolute control over everything but THOUGHT.
- Everything you create begins in the form of a thought.
- Your thoughts create your reality.

14. When You Completely Control Your Thoughts, You Have Victory Over the Fears That Destroy Your Peace

- The control of your thoughts gives you victory over FEAR.

- All thought tends to clothe itself in its physical equivalent.

- It is true, beyond any reasonable room for doubt, that your thoughts create the life of your dreams or nightmares.

- You could choose.

15. Every Human Being and Nation Can Create Poverty and Disease

- The thought impulses of fear and poverty cannot be translated into courage and financial gain.

- The people of America began to think of poverty following the Wall Street Crash of 1929.

- Slowly, but surely that mass thought was crystallized into its physical equivalent the depression."

- This had happened in conformity with the laws of Nature.

16. The Fear of Poverty

- There can be no compromise between POVERTY and RICHES!

- The two roads that lead to poverty and riches travel in opposite directions.

- If you want riches, you must refuse to accept any circumstance that leads to poverty.

17. The Starting Point of The Path That Leads to Riches Is DESIRE

- The word "riches" is used in its broadest sense, meaning financial, spiritual, mental, and material estates.

- The path to riches requires you to make a definite choice to achieve your dreams.

- Luck is not enough to gain the wealth of your dreams and keep it for a lifetime.

18. You Can Turn Prophet and Foretell, Accurately, What the Future Holds in Store for You

- If you are willing to accept poverty, you may as well make up your mind to receive poverty

- This is one decision you cannot avoid.

- If you demand riches, determine what form and how much will be required to satisfy you.

- You know the road that leads to riches, and you must choose it

19. You Can Blame Your Success of Failure on Only One Person, You!

- You have been given a road map.

- If you followed, you would stay on that road.

- If you neglect to start or stop before you arrive, no one will be to blame but YOU.

20. You Have the Responsibility of Deciding If You Are Going to Be a Success or Failure

- This responsibility is yours.

- No alibi will save you from accepting the responsibility if you now fail or refuse to demand riches of life.

- The acceptance calls for incidentally; the only thing you can control is your STATE OF MIND.

21. Your State of Mind Is The most critical Factor in Creating Your Daily Reality and Your Future Success

- Your state of mind cannot be purchased.

- Your state of mind must be created.

- Fear of poverty is a state of mind, nothing else!

22. The Fear of Poverty Grew Out of People's Desire to Gain Wealth and Power at Any Cost Right or Wrong!

- Nothing brings so much suffering and humility as POVERTY!

- Only those who have experienced poverty understand the whole meaning of this.

- It is no wonder that people fear poverty.

23. Fear of Poverty on A National Scale Contributed to the Great Depression Where Millions Lost Everything They Owned Overnight

- Fear of poverty is sufficient to destroy your chances of achievement in any undertaking.

- This truth became painfully evident during the "Great Depression."

24. Fear of Poverty Can Devastate Your Life

- Paralyzes the faculty of reason

- Destroys the faculty of imagination

218

- Kills off self-reliance
- Undermines enthusiasm
- Discourages initiative
- Leads to the uncertainty of purpose
- Encourages procrastination
- Wipes out

25. Fear of Poverty Paralyzes You Until You Cannot Do Anything but Fail

- Makes self-control an impossibility
- Takes the charm from your personality
- Destroys the possibility of accurate thinking
- Diverts concentration of effort
- Destroys persistence
- Turns your willpower into nothingness
- Destroys your ambition

26. Your Fear of Poverty Is Catastrophic to Everyone in Your Life

- Clouds your memory.
- Invites failure in every conceivable form.
- Kills love.
- Assassinates the more delicate emotions of the heart.
- Discourages friendship.
- Invites disaster in a hundred forms.

219

• Leads to sleeplessness, misery, and unhappiness.

27. Fear of Poverty Creates Disease

• Fear of poverty exists in a world of over-abundance of everything the heart could desire, with nothing standing between you and your desires, except lack of a definite purpose.

• The Fear of Poverty is, without doubt, the most destructive of the six basic fears.

28. Fear of Poverty Is Crippling

• It has been placed at the head of the list.

• It is the most difficult to master.

• Considerable courage is required to state the truth about the origin of this fear.

• It requires still more extraordinary courage to accept the truth after it has been exposed.

29. The Fear of Poverty Grew Out of Men and Women's Inherited Tendency to Take Advantage of Their Fellow Citizens Socially and Economically

• Nearly all animals lower than man are motivated by instinct.

• Their capacity to "think" is limited.

• They prey upon one another physically.

• People today have a superior sense of intuition.

30. Fear of Poverty Grew Out of Men and Women's Greed for Money and Their Lust for Power Over Others

• They can think and reason.

- They are not cannibals who eat their opponents.

- They get more satisfaction out of "eating" others FINANCIALLY.

- Many people are so greedy and avaricious that they violate every conceivable law passed to safeguard others.

31. **Money and Material Possessions Are the Total Focus of Some People Who Will Sacrifice Everything to Get What They Want in Any Way Possible**

- People today are made insane because of their money madness.

- Individuals are considered less than the dust of the earth if they do not have a fat bank account.

- Having money is everything, NEVER MIND HOW IT WAS ACQUIRED

32. **Those Who Lust for Wealth and Power Believe They Should Rule in Politics and Dominate Others in Business**

- Money-mad people believe they are above the law.

- They feel they deserve to rule in politics.

- They think they should dominate in business.

- They expect the whole world to bow in respect when they pass.

33. **Through A Long Line of Inherited Experiences, People Learn That some people Cannot Be Trusted in Matters of Money and Earthly Possessions**

- This is a rather stinging indictment.

- The worst part is that it is TRUE.

- Many marriages are motivated by the wealth possessed by one, or both contracting parties

34. Divorce Is Often an Emotional and Financial Battleground Where the Division of Wealth and Material Possessions Determines the Victor at the End of a Failed Relationship

- It is no wonder, therefore, that the divorce courts are busy.

- Some people are so eager to be wealthy they will acquire it in whatever manner they can.

- They will try legal methods if possible but resort to other methods if necessary or expedient.

35. Through A Long Line of Inherited Experiences, People Learn That Some Individuals Cannot Be Trusted in Matters of Money and Earthly Possessions

- Self-analysis will disclose weaknesses you don't want to acknowledge.

- This form of examination is essential if you demand life more than mediocrity and poverty.

36. Remember, As You Check Yourself Point by Point, You Are Both the Court and The Jury, The Prosecuting Attorney and The Attorney for The Defense, And That You Are the Plaintiff And The Defendant, Also You Are On Trial

- Face the facts squarely.

- Ask yourself actual questions and demand direct replies.

37. Are You Willing to Ask Yourself These Questions and Answer Truthfully?

- When the examination is over, you will know more about yourself.

- If you feel that you can be an impartial judge in this self-examination, call someone who knows you well to serve as judge while you cross-examine yourself.

- You are after the truth.

- Get it, no matter at what cost, even though it may temporarily embarrass you!

38. Is "NO FEAR" Your Perspective in Life?

- Many people, if asked what they fear most, would reply, "I fear nothing."

- The reply would be inaccurate.

- Few people realize that they are bound, handicapped, whipped spiritually and physically through some form of fear.

- So subtle and deeply seated is the emotion of fear that you may go through life burdened with it, never recognizing its presence.

39. Only If You Tell Yourself the Truth Will You Come to Know Who You Are

- Only a courageous analysis will disclose the presence of this universal enemy.

- When you begin such an analysis, search deeply into your character.

40. Symptoms of The Fear of Poverty

- Indifference—Lack of ambition – Willingness to tolerate poverty – Acceptance of whatever compensation life may offer without protest – Mental and physical laziness – Lack of initiative, imagination, enthusiasm, and self-control.

41. Symptoms of The Fear of Poverty

- Indecision—Habit of permitting others to do your thinking – Staying "on the fence."

- Doubt – Alibis and excuses designed to cover up, explain away, or apologize for your failures – Envy of those who are successful – Criticizing people who are.

42. Symptoms of The Fear of Poverty

- Worry—Finding fault with others – Tendency to spend beyond your income – Neglect of personal appearance – Scowling and frowning – Intemperance in the use of alcohol or narcotics.

43. Symptoms of The Fear of Poverty

- Worry—Nervousness – Lack of poise – Self-consciousness – Lack of self-reliance

44. Symptoms of The Fear of Poverty

- Over-Caution—Habit of looking for the negative side of every circumstance – Thinking and talking of possible failure instead of concentrating upon the means of succeeding – Knowing all the roads to disaster – Never searching for the plans to avoid failure

45. Symptoms of The Fear of Poverty

- Over-Caution (Continued) – Waiting for "the right time" to begin putting ideas and plans into action until the waiting becomes a permanent habit. – Remembering those who have failed—Forgetting those who have succeeded – Seeing the hole in the doughnut – Overlooking the doughnut – Pessimism that leads to indigestion, poor elimination, auto-intoxication, bad breath, and destructive disposition.

46. Symptoms of The Fear of Poverty

- Procrastination

- Habit of putting off until tomorrow should have been done last year.

- Spending enough time creating alibis and excuses to have done the job.

- Closely related to over-caution, doubt, and worry.

47. Symptoms of The Fear of Poverty
- Refusal to accept responsibility when it can be avoided.

- Willingness to compromise rather than put up a stiff fight, compromising with difficulties instead of harnessing and using them as stepping stones to advancement.

48. Symptoms of The Fear of Poverty
- Bargaining with Life for a penny, instead of demanding prosperity, opulence, riches, contentment, and happiness

- Planning what to do when overtaken by failure, instead of burning all bridges and making retreat impossible

- Weakness of, and often total lack of self-confidence, definiteness of purpose, self-control, initiative, enthusiasm, ambition, thrift, and sound reasoning ability.

49. Symptoms of The Fear of Poverty
- Expecting poverty instead of demanding riches.

- Association with those who accept poverty instead of seeking the company of those who demand and receive riches.

50. Money Talks with Authority
- Why did Napoleon Hill write a book about money?

- Why measure riches in dollars, alone?"

- Some will believe, and rightly so, that there are other forms of riches more desirable than money.

- Yes, some riches cannot be measured in terms of dollars.

- There are millions of people who will say, "Give me all the money I need, and I will find everything else I want.

51. Money Has a Language of Its Own, So You Need to Learn How to Speak Wealth into Your Life
- "Money is only clam shells or metal discs or scraps of paper.

- There are treasures of the heart and soul money cannot buy

- Unfortunately, being broke, most people are unable to keep this in mind and sustain their spirits.

52. Poverty Destroys The human spirit and Is Seen in Your Posture
- Anyone on the streets without a job, unable to find work at all, experiences something that affects their spirit.

- It can be observed in their look, how their shoulders are lowered, and how they walk.

53. Poverty Stricken Individuals Are Society's Human Casualties
- They cannot escape feelings of inferiority with regular employment because they feel they are not equal in character, intelligence, or ability.

- A poor person may borrow for a time, but not enough to carry on in their accustomed way.

- Successful people feel superiority and regard poverty-stricken individuals, perhaps unconsciously, as a casualty.

54. Borrowing Is No Answer When You Need to Earn Money
- They cannot continue to borrow very long.

- Borrowing, when a man is borrowing merely to live, is a depressing experience.

- The money lacks the power of earned money to revive a person's spirits.

- None of this applies to panhandlers or habitual criminals, but only to men of normal ambitions and self-respect.

55. Women Conceal Poverty and Despair Better Than Men
- Women in the same predicament must be different.

- We somehow do not think of women at all in considering the down-and-outers.

- They are scarce in the breadlines.

- They rarely are seen begging on the streets.

56. Women Do Not Make as Much of a Show About Their Dire Straits
- They are not recognizable in crowds by the same plain signs identifying busted men.

- I do not mean the city streets' shuffling hags, which are the opposite number of the confirmed male beggars.

57. Women Deal with Poverty and Despair Secretly
- I mean reasonably young, decent, and intelligent women.

- There must be many of them, but their despair is not apparent.

- Maybe they kill themselves.

- When a man is down and out, he has time on his hands for brooding.

58. Men Will Travel Miles Only to Discover There Is No Job
- He may travel miles to see a man about a job and discover that the position is filled or that it is one of those jobs with no base pay but only a commission on the sale of some useless knick-knack nobody would buy, except out of pity.

- Turning that down, he finds himself back on the street with nowhere to go but just anywhere.

59. Men Will Wander the World in Search of Their Self-Confidence
- So, he walks and walks.

- He gazes into store windows at luxuries that are not for him.

- He feels inferior and gives way to people who stop to look with an active interest.

- He wanders into the railroad station or puts himself down in the library to ease his legs and soak up a little heat.

60. Men May Try to Fool Others by Dressing and Acting Successful

- But that isn't looking for a job, so he gets going again.

- He may not know it, but his aimlessness gives him away even if the very lines of his figure did not.

- He may be well dressed in the clothes left over when he had a steady job, but the clothes cannot disguise the droop.

61. Money Makes a Huge Difference

- "He sees thousands of other people, bookkeepers or clerks or chemists or wagon hands, busy at their work and envies them from the bottom of his soul.

- They have independence, self-respect, and manhood, and he cannot convince himself that he is a good man.

- He argues it out and arrives at a favorable verdict hour after hour.

- It is just money that makes this difference in him

62. Poverty-Stricken Individuals are victimized By Some Employers

- With a bit of money, he would be himself again.

- Some employers take the most shocking advantage of people who are down and out.

- The agencies hang out little colored cards offering miserable wages to busted men.

63. To be fair, men do not always have the same options as women in general. It has become socially acceptable to use social networks and apps to sell themselves as escorts, even though men do it; women dominate this industry. This assessment does not include sex trafficking, which is another nature of its own. But the internet is plagued with porn, dating, and escorts that have changed our society since Napoleon Hill's writings about fears. And it's all about fear of lack and loss — others for just lust of pleasure and others greed of money.
https://www.slideshare.net/biomans/napoleon-hill-in-think-and-grow-rich-discusses-the-destructive-power-of-fear

CHAPTER 18

FEAR OF FAILURE

Here are the 30 major causes of failure according to Think and Grow Rich:

1. Unfavorable Hereditary background

If you have some deficiency of brainpower because of a disability or some sort, you cannot do much about it. This is the only one of the 30 causes of failure that cannot be easily corrected. But a better understanding of the mind today has offered hope and opportunities through positive research.

2. Lack of a well-defined purpose in life

If you don't have some goal you aim for, how are you supposed to achieve anything or be successful? Have a clear, defined plan that you want to achieve and know why you are working to reach it.

3. Lack of ambition to aim above mediocrity

People who don't want to get ahead in life can never be successful. This is when you don't want to improve your life and stay at a mediocre level. I doubt most people intend to remain mediocre their entire lives.

4. Insufficient education

A lack of proper education can be overcome with ease. In Think and Grow Rich, Napoleon Hill explains that it is not so much the most highly educated people in school that are the most successful, but the ones who self-educate themselves. School cannot teach you experience. It is not all about knowledge, but the knowledge that is applied that is important.

5. Lack of self-discipline

If you step in front of the mirror and feel like you see your greatest enemy, this may be one of your most prominent causes of failure. You must learn self-control to avoid letting any negative qualities overtake you. You must develop your mind and become your own best friend to conquer yourself this way.

6. Ill health

If you aren't healthy, you probably don't ever feel like getting much work done. Unfortunately, this is another aspect of self-control that many people struggle with. The five leading causes of ill health outlined in the book are:

a. Overeating foods that don't promote good health

b. The wrong expression of thought; indicating negatives

c. Inappropriate use of and overindulgence in sex

d. Lack of regular physical exercise

e. Improper breathing, causing an inadequate supply of fresh air

7. Unfavorable environmental influences during childhood

One thing you cannot do is live in the past.

"If you drive with a rear-view mirror, you're going to crash."

-Tony Robbins

Most people that become criminals had terrible childhoods or just grew up in a bad environment. However, many have been through this and overcome it, so others must learn to succeed by surrounding themselves with the right supportive people.

8. Procrastination

Procrastination is one of the biggest causes of failure. It's one of the ones I struggled with the most when starting as an entrepreneur. But unfortunately, it seems that people are becoming lazier and lazier as technology progresses today.

"This does not promote success. Instead, hard work and consistency are what will get you to where you want to go."

9. Lack of persistence

It's a lot easier to start something than it is to finish it. Especially in entrepreneurship, people tend to be excited about getting started but then quit at the first sign of defeat. The most successful people in the world had to go through many failures before their first successes.

Failure cannot cope with persistence. However, if you consistently work towards something, you will get past every bump in the road you hit and eventually reach success.

10. Negative personality

It would be best if you attracted people to you with your personality, not repel them. When people are attracted to you, they want to do business with you and be around you. Therefore, to become a more positive person, you will develop better relationships with people who can help you.

11. Lack of controlled sexual urge

Sex is the most potent stimuli that move people to action. It must be controlled, and the emotional energy must be converted into other channels.

12. Uncontrolled desire for "something for nothing."

To reach success or achieve any goal, you must provide something in exchange. To always want something for nothing is to have a gambler's mentality that will never reward you in life consistently. Instead, it would be best if you gave value to get value in return.

"An example of how the gambling instinctive causes failure is the stock market crash of 1929."

13. Lack of a well-defined power of decision

Business owners can make the most challenging decisions under pressure because they make quick decisions and change their minds slowly. On the other hand, failures make slow decisions, if any, and change their minds too quickly.

"You can't stay consistent if you keep changing your mind on the direction you're going in."

14. One or more of the six basic fears

It will help if you overcome any fears that may hold you back from achieving a goal.

15. Wrong selection of a mate in marriage

It's a sad statistic, but more people in the U.S. live now divorced than married. Many people do not have a harmonious marriage, and that can affect business or work performance. Being unhappy in your personal life will usually kill your ambition for achieving great things in your career. We can accredit most of this divorcing from the contribution from entertainment providing a stimulate for lust to incubate into desire other than your spouse. Our priorities and commitment to family are misplaced. Usually, the children become the outcast and hurt without consideration from the separation. When it becomes less about you and more about the children's mental, physical health, and welfare, maybe you will understand the damage you can cause.

16. Over-caution

Although you don't want to be too hasty, you don't want to be overly cautious. You must take some chances to achieve big things, but don't go for the hail Mary every time. Make logical decisions, and you'll have a good balance of caution and risk.

17. Wrong selection of associates in business

If you're going to work with others in your industry, you want them to be people to uplift you. So, if you choose an employer, try to choose one that is an inspiration and sets an excellent example for you to learn.

18. Superstition and prejudice

A superstition is a form of ignorance, and so is being prejudiced. A superstition is also a form of fear. Successful people keep open minds and are afraid of nothing.

19. Wrong selections of a vocation

It's hard to strive to achieve great things in a field you aren't very passionate about. But, on the other hand, it's incredible how many people settle for less and take a job they don't even like because they think they have no choice.

20. Lack of a concentration of effort

You don't want to try and master too many things all at once. Become a specialist before you branch out into other things because a "jack-of-all-trades" isn't very good at anything.

"I fear not the man who practiced 10,000 kicks once. I fear the man who practiced one kick 10,000 times."

– Bruce Lee

21. The habit of indiscriminate spending

Especially in business, you need to have a budget. You need to be able to manage money in all aspects of life. Indiscriminate spending will create a fear of poverty because you won't ever have much money left over in the bank. Without much money in the bank, you won't have much courage to push for better business deals. So, you take whatever you are offered when you have a fear of going broke.

22. Lack of enthusiasm

Have you ever tried to do a business deal or sell something when you didn't even have any enthusiasm about what you were selling? If so, you know it never goes very well. People don't like downers. Get around enthusiastic people about what they're doing, and it'll rub off on you.

23. Intolerance

You don't want to be closed-minded when trying to achieve success. Instead, it would help if you were open to new strategies and knowledge from those who have already reached the level you want to be.

24. Intemperance

Napoleon Hill states that it could be fatal to your success if you overindulge in things like food, sex, or drinking. So, control yourself and don't give in to little temptations that could throw you off track.

25. Inability to cooperate with others

If you do not know how to deal with people or work well with others, you will rarely become successful in any situation. You're not always going to be correct. You're not always going to get your way. Learn to accept that and be tolerant of other people, and you're already way ahead of countless others in the journey to success.

26. Possession of power that was not acquired through self-effort

Have you ever noticed that many people that get large inheritances at an early age or people that win the lottery tend to blow all the money, only to be broke again? Successful people stay successful because they earned their success and created a mindset of total commitment and the secret of a singleness of purpose.

27. Intentional dishonesty

Your word and reputation can be your most significant assets or biggest faults when moving up in life. But, unfortunately, being dishonest with people on purpose is an excellent way to get in peoples' "doghouse" and end up losing everything.

28. Egotism and vanity

These two things are just fatal to success. When people see these traits in you, they are red flags that are hard to look past.

29. Guessing instead of thinking

Have you ever known one of those people that automatically makes arguments and forms opinions on the spot without even taking the time to learn the facts? That won't win you much respect in life either. Be logical and know the facts before making decisions or forming opinions. Laziness and not doing your homework will lead to a lot of wrong judgments.

30. Lack of capital

Especially when it comes to starting a business for the first time, it helps to have some money in the bank to absorb the mistakes you're likely to make and keep you from getting into debt, killing your credit, or anything like that. But, unfortunately, those types of problems are hard to recover from in today's world. Even more so in the minority communities, it seems as it's a corporate conspiracy.

THE FEAR OF LOSS OF LOVE

Since man's polygamous habit of stealing his fellow man's mate, as well as his tendency to take liberties with her whenever he could, is the source of this inherent fear, a little description is needed. It is derived from man's inherited fear of losing a love that the disease of jealousy and other similar forms of dementia praecox develop. This fear is the most painful of all the six basic fears. It probably plays more havoc with the body and mind than any other basic fears, as it often leads to permanent insanity.

The fear of losing love probably dates to the stone age, when men stole women by brute force. They continue to steal females, but their technique has changed. Instead of power, they now use persuasion, the promise of pretty clothes, motor cars, and other "bait" much more effective than physical force. Man's habits are the same as at the dawn of civilization, but he expresses them differently.

Careful analysis has shown that women are more susceptible to this fear than men. This fact is easily explained. Women have learned, from experience, that men are polygamous by nature, that they are not to be trusted in the hands of rivals.

SYMPTOMS OF THE FEAR OF LOSS OF LOVE

The distinctive symptoms of this fear are:

JEALOUSY: The habit of being suspicious of friends and loved ones without any reasonable evidence of sufficient grounds. (Jealousy is a form of dementia praecox, which sometimes becomes violent without the slightest cause). The habit of accusing wife or husband of infidelity without grounds. General suspicion of everyone, absolute faith in no one.

FAULT FINDING: The habit of finding fault with friends, relatives, business associates, and loved ones upon the slightest provocation or without any cause whatsoever.

GAMBLING: The habit of gambling, stealing, cheating, and otherwise taking hazardous chances to provide money for loved ones, with the belief that love can be bought. The habit of spending beyond one's means, or incurring debts, delivers gifts for loved ones, with the object of making a good showing. Can't sleep, nervousness, persistence, weakness of will, lack of self-control, self-reliance, bad temper.

THE FEAR OF DEATH

To some, this is the cruelest of all the basic fears. The reason is apparent. In most cases, the terrible pangs of anxiety associated with the thought of death may be charged directly to religious fanaticism. So-called "heathens" are less afraid of death than the more "civilized." For hundreds of millions of years, man has been asking the still unanswered questions, "whence" and "whither." (I do not accept this statement referring to the time, but I didn't change Napoleon Hill's words.)

Where did I come from, and where am I going? During the darker ages of the past, the more cunning and crafty were not slow to offer the answer to these questions, FOR A PRICE— Witness, now, the primary source of origin of the FEAR OF DEATH.

"Come into my tent, embrace my faith, accept my dogmas, and I will give you a ticket that will admit you straightaway into heaven when you die," cries a leader of sectarianism. "Remain out of my tent," says the same leader, "and may the devil take you and burn you throughout eternity."

ETERNITY is a long time. FIRE is a terrible thing. The thought of eternal punishment, with fire, causes man to fear death, which often causes him to lose his reason. It destroys interest in life and makes happiness impossible. During my research, I reviewed a book entitled "A Catalogue of the Gods," which listed the 30,000 gods that man has worshiped. Think of it! Thirty thousand of them, represented by everything from a crawfish to a man. It is little wonder that men have become frightened at the approach of death.

While the religious leader may not be able to provide safe conduct into heaven, nor, by lack of such provision, allow the unfortunate to descend into hell, the possibility of the latter seems so terrible. So realistically, the very thought lays hold of the imagination that paralyzes reason and sets up the fear of death.

In truth, NO MAN KNOWS, and no man has ever known, what heaven or hell is like, nor does any man know if either place exists. This very lack of positive knowledge opens the door of the human mind to the charlatan so he may enter and control that mind with his stock of legerdemain and various brands of pious fraud and trickery.

241

The fear of DEATH is not as common now as when there were no great colleges and universities. Men of science have turned the spotlight of truth upon the world, and this truth is rapidly freeing men and women from this terrible fear of DEATH. The young men and women who attend the colleges and universities are not easily impressed by "fire" and "brimstone."

Through the aid of biology, astronomy, geology, and other related sciences, the fears of the dark ages that gripped men's minds and destroyed their reason have been dispelled. Nevertheless, insane asylums are overflowing with men and women who have gone mad because of the FEAR OF DEATH.

This fear is useless. Death will come, no matter what anyone may think about it. Accept it as a necessity and pass the thought out of your mind. It must be a necessity, or it would not come to all. Perhaps it is not as bad as it has been pictured.

The entire world is made up of only two things, ENERGY and MATTER. In elementary physics, we learn that neither matter nor energy (the only two realities known to man) can be created nor destroyed. Both matter and energy can be transformed, but neither can be eliminated.

Life is energy if it is anything. If neither energy nor matter can be destroyed, of course, life cannot be destroyed. Like other forms of energy, life may be passed through various processes of transition or change, but it cannot be destroyed.

Death is a mere transition. If death is not mere change or transition, nothing comes after death except a long, eternal, peaceful sleep, and sleep is nothing to be feared. Thus, you may wipe out, forever, the fear of death.

SYMPTOMS OF THE FEAR OF DEATH

The general symptoms of this fear are the habit of THINKING about dying instead of making the most of LIFE, due, generally, to lack of purpose or absence of a suitable occupation. This fear is more prevalent among the aged, but sometimes the more youthful are victims of it. The greatest of all remedies for fear of death is a BURNING DESIRE FOR ACHIEVEMENT, backed by helpful service to others. A busy person seldom has time to think about dying. He finds life too thrilling to worry about death. Sometimes the fear of death is closely associated with the Fear of Poverty, where one's death would leave loved ones poverty-stricken. In other cases, the fear of death is caused by illness and the consequent breaking down of physical body resistance. The most typical causes of the fear of death are ill -health, poverty, lack of appropriate occupation, disappointment over love, insanity, religious fanaticism.

OLD MAN WORRY

Worry is a state of mind based upon fear. It works slowly but persistently. It is insidious and subtle. Step by step, it "digs itself in" until it paralyzes one's reasoning faculty, destroys self-confidence and initiative. A worry is a form of sustained fear caused by indecision; therefore, it is a state of mind control. An unsettled mind is helpless. Uncertainty makes an agitated mind. Most individuals lack the willpower to promptly reach decisions and stand by them after being made, even during normal business conditions. During periods of economic unrest (such as the world recently experienced), the individual is disabled, not alone by his inherent nature to be slow at reaching decisions, but he is influenced by the indecision of others around him who have created a state; of "mass indecision."

243

During the depression, the whole atmosphere, all over the world, was filled with "Fearenza" and "Worryitis," the two mental disease germs which began to spread themselves after the Wall Street frenzy in 1929. There is only one known antidote for these germs; it is the habit of prompt and firm DECISION. Moreover, it is an antidote that every individual must apply for himself. We do not worry over conditions once we have decided to follow a definite line of action.

I once interviewed a man who was to be electrocuted two hours later. The condemned man was the calmest of some eight men who were in the death cell with him. His calmness prompted me to ask him how it felt to know that he was going into eternity in a short while. With a smile of confidence on his face, he said, "It feels fine.

Just think, brother, my troubles will soon be over. I have had nothing but trouble all my life. It has been a hardship to get food and clothing. Soon I will not need these things. I have felt fine ever since I learned FOR CERTAIN that I must die. I made up my mind then to accept my fate in good spirit." As he spoke, he devoured a dinner of proportions sufficient for three men, eating every mouthful of the food brought to him and enjoying it as much as if no disaster awaited him.

The decision gave this man resignation to his fate! A decision can also prevent one's acceptance of undesired circumstances. The six basic fears become translated into a state of worry through indecision. Relieve yourself, forever of the fear of death, by deciding to accept death as an inescapable event — whip the fear of poverty by choosing to get along with whatever wealth you can accumulate WITHOUT WORRY. Put your foot upon the neck of the fear of criticism by deciding NOT TO WORRY about what other people think, do, or say. Eliminate the fear of old age by choosing to accept it, not as a handicap, but as a great blessing that carries with it wisdom, self-control, and understanding not known to youth.

Acquit yourself of the fear of ill health by the decision to forget symptoms. Master the fear of losing love by deciding to get along without love, if necessary. In all its forms, kill the habit of worry by contacting a general, blanket decision that nothing life has to offer is worth the price of anxiety. With this decision will come poise, peace of mind, and calmness of thought, bringing happiness. A man whose mind is filled with fear not only destroys his chances of intelligent action, but he transmits these destructive vibrations to the minds of all who encounter him and destroys their chances.

Even a dog or a horse knows when its master lacks courage; moreover, a dog or horse will pick up the vibrations of fear thrown off by its master and behave accordingly. Lower down the intelligence line in the animal kingdom; one finds this same capacity to pick up the vibrations of fear. For example, a honeybee immediately senses fear in a person's mind for unknown reasons; a bee will sting the person whose mind releases vibrations of fear much more readily than it will molest the person whose mind registers no fear.

The vibrations of fear pass from one mind to another just as quickly and as indeed as the sound of the human voice passes from the broadcasting station to the receiving set of a radio-and BY THE SELF-SAME MEDIUM.

Patrick Barber Sr.

THE FEAR OF CRITICISM

Just as the man originally came by this fear, no one can state it, but one thing is sure- he has it in a highly developed form. Some believe that this fear made its appearance around the time that politics became a "profession." Others think it can be traced to when women first began to concern themselves with "styles" in wearing apparel.

Since this author is neither a humorist nor a prophet, he tends to believe that man's inherited nature is what causes him to take away his fellowman's goods and wares and CRITICIZE his character. It is a well-known fact that a thief will criticize the man from whom he steals-that politicians seek office, not by displaying their virtues and qualifications, but by attempting to besmirch their opponents.

The fear of criticism takes on many forms, the majority of which are petty and trivial. Bald men, for example, are bald for no other reason than their fear of criticism. Heads become bald because of the tight-fitting bands of hats, which cut off the circulation from the roots of the hair. Men wear hats, not because they need them, but mainly because "everyone is doing it. The individual falls into line and does likewise, lest some other individuals CRITICIZE him. Women seldom have bald heads, or even thin hair, because they wear hats that fit their heads loosely, the only purpose of the caps being adornment.

But it must not be supposed that women are free from the fear of criticism. If any woman claims to be superior to a man regarding this fear, ask her to walk down the street wearing a hat of the vintage of 1890. The astute manufacturers of clothing have not been slow to capitalize on this basic fear of criticism, with which all humanity has been cursed. Every season the styles in many articles of wearing apparel change. Who establishes the styles? Indeed, not the purchaser of clothing, but the manufacturer. Why does he change the styles so often? The answer is obvious. He changes the styles so he can sell more clothes.

For the same reason, the manufacturers of automobiles (with a few rare and very sensible exceptions) change models every season. No man wants to drive a car not of the latest style, although the older model may be better. We have described how people behave under the influence of fear of criticism applied to life's small and petty things. Let us examine human behavior when this fear affects people connected with the more important events of human relationships. Take, for example, practically any person who has reached the age of "mental maturity" (from 35 to 40 years of age, as a general average). If you could read the secret thoughts of his mind, you would find a very decided disbelief in most of the fables taught by many of the dogmatists and theologians a few decades back.

Not often, however, will you find a person who dares to state his belief on this subject openly. If pressed far enough, most people will tell a lie rather than admit that they do not believe the stories associated with that form of religion that held people in bondage before the age of scientific discovery and education. Why does the average person, even in this day of enlightenment, shy away from denying his belief in the fables, which were the basis of most religions a few decades ago? The answer is, "because of the fear of criticism." Men and women have been burned at stake for daring to express disbelief in ghosts. It is no wonder we have inherited a consciousness that makes us fear criticism. The time was not so far in the past when criticism carried severe punishments-it still does in some countries.

The fear of criticism robs man of his initiative, destroys his power of imagination, limits his individuality, takes away his self-reliance, and does his damage in a hundred other ways. Parents often do their children irreparable injury by criticizing them. The mother of one of my boyhood chums used to punish him with a switch almost daily, always completing the job with the statement, "You'll land in the penitentiary before you are twenty." He was sent to a Reformatory at the age of seventeen. Criticism is the one form of service of which everyone has too much. Everyone has a stock of it which is handed out, gratis, whether called for or not.

One's nearest relatives often are the worst offenders. It should be recognized as a crime (in reality, a corruption of the worst nature) for any parent to build inferiority complexes in a child's mind through unnecessary criticism — employers who understand human nature get the best in men, not by criticism but by constructive suggestion. Parents may accomplish the same results with their children. Criticism will plant FEAR in the human heart or resentment, but it will not build love or affection.

SYMPTOMS OF THE FEAR OF CRITICISM; This fear is almost as universal as the fear of poverty. Its effects are just as fatal to personal achievement, mainly because this fear destroys initiative and discourages imagination.

SELF-CONSCIOUSNESS. It is expressed through nervousness, timidity in conversation, meeting strangers, awkward movement of the hands and limbs, and shifting eyes.

LACK OF POISE. It is expressed through lack of voice control, nervousness in the presence of others, poor posture of the body, poor memory.

PERSONALITY. They lack firmness of decision, personal charm, and the ability to express opinions. It is a habit that causes one to side-step issues instead of meeting them squarely and agreeing with others without carefully examining their views.

INFERIORITY COMPLEX. The habit of expressing self-approval by word of mouth and by actions means covering up a feeling of inferiority and using "big words" to impress others (often without knowing the real meaning of the words), and imitating others in dress, speech, and manners and boasting of imaginary achievements. This sometimes gives a surface appearance of a feeling of superiority.

EXTRAVAGANCE. The habit of trying to "keep up with the Jones's" spending beyond one's income.

LACK OF INITIATIVE. Failure to embrace opportunities for self-advancement, fear to express opinions, lack of confidence in one's ideas, giving evasive an-were to questions asked by superiors, the hesitancy of manner and speech, deceit in both words and deeds.

LACK OF AMBITION. Mental and physical laziness, lack of self-assertion, slow-ness in reaching decisions, easily influenced by others, the habit of criticizing others behind their backs and flattering them to their faces, the practice of accepting defeat without protest, quitting an undertaking when opposed by others, suspicious of other people without cause, lacking in tactfulness of manner and speech, unwillingness to accept the blame for mistakes.

THE FEAR OF OLD AGE

In the mind, this fear grows out of two sources. First, the thought that old age may bring with it POVERTY. Secondly, and by far the most common source of origin, from false and cruel teachings of the past which have been too well mixed with "fire and brimstone," and other bogies cunningly designed to enslave man through fear.

An apprehension of old age is rooted in two very valid motives. In the first case, he distrusts those who may seize any worldly goods he may possess, and, in the other, he has dreaded the world beyond. This was the mindset he had before he could truly grasp his thoughts. The possibility of ill health, which is more common as people grow older, is also a contributing cause of this common fear of old age. Further, when a man is conscious of decreasing sexual appeal, this decrease is also a contributing factor. The most common cause of fear of old age is associated with the possibility of poverty. "Poorhouse" is not a pretty word. But it throws a chill into the mind of every person who faces the possibility of having to spend his declining years on a poor farm.

Another contributing cause of the fear of old age is the possibility of losing freedom and independence, as old age may bring with it the loss of both physical and economic freedom.

SYMPTOMS OF THE FEAR OF OLD AGE

The most typical symptoms of this fear are:

The tendency to slow down and develop an inferiority complex at the age of mental maturity, around forty, falsely believing oneself to be "slipping" because of age when the truth is that man's most useful years, mentally and spiritually, are those between forty and sixty. Thus, instead of reversing the rule and expressing gratitude for having reached the age of wisdom and understanding, the habit of speaking apologetically of oneself as "being old" merely because one has reached the age of forty or fifty.

The habit of killing off initiative, imagination, and self-reliance by falsely believing oneself too old to exercise these qualities. The practice of the man or woman of forty dressing to try to appear much younger and affecting mannerisms of youth: thereby inspiring ridicule by both friends and strangers.

THE EGO

Definition of EGO; a person who is preoccupied with his interests; a selfish person. An arrogant person; egotist. Ego is a prefix that describes a person's sense of self-importance or their sense of importance to others. Having an inflated sense of value is the definition of egotism - thinking one is better than others. Someone who is egotistical is full of himself, completely self-absorbed. Whenever they have a point of view, they always try to defend it without reasoning or empathy.

EGO GATEKEEPER

The administrator of all actions is also the autoresponder.

One thing is for sure the ego is full of pride and Lust. It houses everything related to the flesh and self-preservation; it lacks empathy and compassion most of the time. It has a total disregard for the thoughts and well-being of others. It's all about what's in it for me. He stands at the front door of the mind seeking to strike against anyone that fails to submit to its needs or desires. As soon as the conscious mind receives input, the subconscious mind gets an instant deposit. This deposit is unfiltered for data quality; it accepts whatever is sent and cannot reject it.

Take every thought into captivity—the importance of controlling your thoughts is to avoid negative input contrary to the principles and morals of your belief. Whatever you allow released into your subconscious has the possibility of creating irreparable damage to your character. Your five senses are the sensor for more than just sight, touch, taste, hearing, and smell. They are the monitors that feed vibrations to the core of your body. Vibrations determine how you feel, and feeling controls everything; all your actions are reactions of the emotions feedback by the vibrations. An example will be if you don't feel good about something, you won't do it.

Every word should be held in captivity because words are physical beings, just as holding a hammer. They alone have the power to bless or curse. Depending on your faith or core belief system, the word itself means the creation of higher intelligence. That word is the power of the speaker. Whatever word is spoken can become what is believed. The subconscious mind is just like a backlink into a mainframe computer network powering a supercomputer. It continues trying to bridge the gap until the connection is made. It will not stop until it has a satisfactory resolution by the sender. Whatever image it sees, it goes out to complete it is the builder of the imagination, and imagination the builder of our world.

Only allow images of what you want as the results in your conscious mind because the subconscious begins to build whatever you release into its vault. We can ask what we want through a perfect world in our faith, and we would get it. You have that world when you have the proper relationship and understanding of the relationship you have. This is KEY, and where all power to do any and everything begins. But always be mindful that your EGO is on the prowl seeking the opportunity to rebuff everything. It is proud and boastful.

CHAPTER 19

RELIGION CAN BE A DANGEROUS THING, BE CAREFUL WHAT YOU CONSUME

You will always be weak and lacking in the power of your faith if you misunderstand your relationship with the Comforter. Today's new generational phrase means "Infinite Intelligence," without this power; you will always remain defeated. When you misunderstand your relationship with the Holy Spirit, Satan will always use deception to keep you weak, without the power of faith the Holy Spirit gives you. Therefore, Jesus asks the father to send the Comforter on his behalf to re-establish the broken connection from Adam's disobedience in the garden through the Comforter.

We become the image of God when we repent and are born again; just as Adam lost the image of God that moment through disobedience, we gain it for being born again. When the Spirit descended upon Jesus after John baptized him, God said, This is my beloved son in whom I am well pleased. When we are born again, we become the children of God and the apple of his eye.

Acts 1:8

New International Version

8 But you will receive power when the Holy Spirit comes on you, and you will be my witnesses in Jerusalem, and in all Judea and Samaria, and to the ends of the earth.

***

Satan and his servants can masquerade as 'light,' so we are more easily tricked. You must know why you are here and understand your purpose. None of us are here to exist without purpose. But your weapons are not carnal; they are supernatural when we believe in what we receive.

Believers today suffer from their Egos and Pride. We are Three-part beings, whereby the flesh is constantly waring against the Spirit just as Satan wars against God.

We intend to be a Potent DISRUPTOR of religious culture.

The Torah is primarily a covenant between God and the people of Israel. The Torah contains history and God's laws given to the Israelites during the 40 years of the Exodus. There are 613 commands given to the Israelites, but the best-known of these laws are the ten commandments.

The Torah helped create a sense of national identity while living in foreign lands. The Torah represents a common heritage for people to relate to the same belief. The Torah kept national pride alive while being oppressed. It is the most sacred writing of ancient Israelites and modern Jews.

The Torah is also vital for Christians. It teaches us the history of the Israelites and why a savior is needed. The New Testament teaches Old Testament events, and many Old Testament prophecies in the New Testament are complete. Understanding the Old Testament is not a prerequisite for salvation. Still, it can help understand parts of the New Testament whereby Jesus fulfills all the laws and brings a new covenant.

ANCIENT BIBLES
OLD TESTAMENT, NEW TESTAMENT, APOCRYPHA

Some scholars believe there are two ancient Bibles (including the Old Testament, New Testaments, and Apocrypha), which might have been part of the 50 Bibles Emperor Constantine asked to be produced. Codex Vaticanus has been dated to A.D. 300-3257 and stored in the Vatican library since at least 1481 when installed on an index; no one knows when it initially arrived at the Vatican. Codex Sinaiticus recorded A.D. 330-360. The Codex was discovered in several parts between 1844 and 1859 and is currently in four locations, with the most prominent feature at the British Library. I will likely write articles about these manuscripts in the future.

The source claims Constantine created the canon, but the Vetus Synodicon was more than 500 years after the council. So, if atheists can trust this claim in a book written 500 years after the panel, why don't they trust the New Testament books, written less than 50 years after the events and written by eyewitnesses?

Before Constantine's legalizing Christianity, Christians were best tolerated in the Roman Empire and sometimes persecuted (Persecution of the Christians in the Roman Empire). Some emperors before Constantine actively arrested, tortured, and executed Christians (and people of other non-Roman Empire-approved faiths) and had their religious books destroyed. Only after Constantine legalized Christianity that the books of the Bible became widely available to many churches. Constantine did have a tremendous, positive impact on Christianity, but he had nothing to do with forming the New Testament Canon.

CHAPTER 20

VATICAN 14 BOOKS REMOVED

1 4 books were removed from the Bible by the Vatican in 1684 without explanation

However, when this book was original, it contained 80 books, and current editions only have 66, and we must wonder what exact purpose the removal of 14 books would serve?

The first English translation of the Bible was made in 1611. This "original" Bible contained 80 books, including the Apocrypha, which means hidden.

As part of the Old Testament, the Apocrypha books included the following texts:

- **1 Esdras**

- **2 Esdras**

- **Tobit**

- **Judith**

- **The rest of Esther**

- **The Wisdom of Solomon**

- **Ecclesiasticus**

- **Baruch with the epistle Jeremiah**

- **The Songs of the 3 Holy children**

- **The history of Susana**

- **Bel and the Dragon**

- **The prayer for Manasses**

- **1 Maccabees**

- **2 Maccabees**

Later in 1684, The Bible had all other versions removed. The 1611 edition was the only one left intact. So here we see man decided to remove other scriptural text at his discretion and his emotional truth as guidance authorized by God without anyone to challenge this authority. So he was at liberty to deceive a nation of faith wherever it may be. This is why you need the comforter who is all truth. He teaches you and guides you in all things about God.

THE STORY OF THE MOUNTAIN RUNNER

A runner determined to be the greatest, a STORY TESTING TRUE FAITH created a routine that built stamina for when the long-distance race began to take its toll on the runner's energy. Every day he would get up and go to the enormous mountain base and run around it twice and just as he would feel the stresses of running, he would run up the narrow trail on the mountain leading to the top. He knew the path very well and knew it every step of the way, this day. However, he felt he needed to push faster and harder; he got almost to the top, and the trail was a little damp from the climate dew, making the track more slippery than usual.

Then, just as he turned the corner, a squirrel ran down the mountain across his path; caught off guard, he lost his focus and misstep and fell over the side of the trail. The fall would have been 15 stories or more had it not been for a tree limb sticking out from the side. He was able to reach for whatever was in the path on the way down. He held on for dear life and began to scream at the top of his voice, for he knew he was way up, and rarely anyone came that far on the trail.

He felt somewhat hopeless and screamed louder and louder, hoping someone would come to his aid. Then, he began to think about what his family will do, what about his wife and children, how anyone would find him. So, after a while of screaming to no one hearing him, he began to whimper slowly in the realization he may die on the cliff. Then, he remembered his mother and father taught him how to pray to God, and they had introduced him to Christ at an early age. So, he prayed and asked God to help and please send an angel.

So soon as he had finished praying, along came a man and reached over the side with a long stick and told him to grab hold and he would pull him up. He refused because he said, no, you don't look strong enough, I don't have much strength left, and I may slip. So, the man calls for paramedics, then a helicopter arrives and throws down a ladder; he says, no, I want to hang on. So, he screams, Lord help me, and about that time, he heard an audible voice, my child, I am with you, if you believe I am with you, then I am in you. Do you trust and believe in me? He said yes, and God ask again do you trust me, but more importantly, do you believe? He said yes, God said let go. So, he thought for a few seconds, and he started to scream even louder, asking for anyone to help him.

For the believers:

This is the mindset of the believers today; they have a form of Godliness but deny the power of the Holy Spirit inside of them. They only see the operations of the Spirit from working outside and not inside. He is alive with all Power in you.

There is Father, Son and Holy Spirit, and Mind, Body, and Spirit. (Where the comforter lives).